SAN FRANCISCO with KIDS

by Clark Norton, Denise M. Leto

3rd EDITION

FODOR'S TRAVEL PUBLICATIONS

New York * Toronto * London * Sydney * Auckland

www.fodors.com

CREDITS

Writers: Clark Norton, Denise M. Leto
Editor: Paul Eisenberg
Editorial Production: Evangelos Vasilakis
Production/Manufacturing: Angela L. McLean
Design: Fabrizio La Rocca, *creative director;*
Tigist Getachew, *art director*
Cover Art and Design: Jessie Hartland
Flip Art and Illustration and Series Design: Rico Lins,
Keren Ora Admoni/Rico Lins Studio

ABOUT THE WRITERS

Clark Norton, author of *Fodor's Where Should We Take the Kids?: California,* has won two Gold Awards from the Pacific Asia Travel Association for his journalism. He has two children, son Grael and daughter Lia, both born and reared in San Francisco.

Denise M. Leto, who revised the third edition of *Around San Francisco with Kids,* has been mining San Francisco's back streets for more than a dozen years to share the city's ever-changing flavor and hidden gems with other travelers. A longtime contributor to and editor of many Fodor's guidebooks, she shares her love of local lore with her two young, homeschooled sons, who can tell you the story behind Coit Tower and point out the city's original shoreline.

FODOR'S AROUND SAN FRANCISCO WITH KIDS

Third Edition
ISBN 978-1-4000-1920-5
ISSN 1526-1395

AN IMPORTANT TIP AND AN INVITATION

Although all prices, opening times, and other details in this book are based on information supplied to us at press time, changes occur all the time in the travel world, and Fodor's cannot accept responsibility for facts that become outdated or for inadvertent errors or omissions. So always confirm information when it matters, especially if you're making a detour to visit a specific place. Your experiences—positive and negative—matter to us. If we have missed or misstated something, please write to us. We follow up on all suggestions. Contact the Around San Francisco with Kids editor at editors@fodors.com or c/o Fodor's at 1745 Broadway, New York, New York 10019.

SPECIAL SALES

This book is available at special discounts for bulk purchases for sales promotions or premiums. Special editions, including personalized covers, excerpts of existing books, and corporate imprints, can be created in large quantities for special needs. For more information, write to Special Markets/Premium Sales, 1745 Broadway, New York, NY 10019, or e-mail specialmarkets@randomhouse.com.

PRINTED IN THE UNITED STATES OF AMERICA
10 9 8 7 6 5 4 3 2 1

COUNTDOWN TO GOOD TIMES

GET READY, GET SET!

Between drop-offs, pickups, and after-school activities, organizing your family's schedule can seem like a full-time job. Planning for some fun time together shouldn't have to be another. That's where this book helps out. We've done all the legwork, so you don't have to. Open to any page and you'll find a great family activity in the San Francisco Bay Area already planned out. You can read about the main events—most within San Francisco or a short drive away (none more than 90 minutes from the city)—check our age-appropriateness ratings to make sure it's right for your family, pick up some insider tips, and find out where to grab a bite nearby.

To suit most any family's interests and needs, we've included a balance of attractions. You'll find things to do indoors and out, destinations that range from world famous to off the beaten path, events that will fill a day or just a few hours, and activities that appeal to a variety of ages (including parents!). Most of the 68 things to do are available year-round, though some are seasonal (days and hours are listed). And though some of the places, such as theme parks, will take a crunch from your wallet, many others are inexpensive—or even free.

HOW TO SAVE MONEY
Taking a family on an outing can be pricey, but there are ways to save.

1. Think beyond theme parks. Although an amusement or theme park can be a great treat, you can have plenty of fun with your kids without dropping $40 a head. The

Bay Area has priceless natural treasures—such as Muir Woods National Monument and Point Reyes National Seashore—that cost little or nothing to visit. Urban parks (such as San Francisco's Golden Gate Park or Presidio National Park) are other great bargains, as are historic sites, wildlife refuges, and many museums.

2. Watch for discounts, coupons, and passes. Ask about discounts at ticket booths; your affiliation (and an ID) may get you a break. Consider buying season passes. At some theme parks, they may cost only as much as two or three one-day admissions. Many attractions also give discounts for consecutive-day visits or for buying combination tickets to sister attractions (such as Six Flags Discovery Kingdom and Waterworld California). Family memberships to some institutions pay off if you visit more than once or twice. Coupons, meanwhile, can save you up to $4 a ticket at certain attractions; look for them online, in hotels, supermarkets, government tourism offices, even your pediatrician's office. Also watch for special tourist-oriented passes such as CityPass ($54 for adults, $39 for children ages 5–17), which includes free entrance to six San Francisco attractions (you must visit all within nine days), as well as provide a one-week unlimited Muni transit pass, which includes cable cars—and at $5 per ride, that's a huge bonus.

3. Try to go on free days. Several places in this book (such as the California Academy of Sciences, Legion of Honor, the Exploratorium, and the San Francisco Museum of Modern Art) offer free admission on certain days of the week or month.

4. Consider becoming a member of a zoo or art or science museum. Joining usually costs $50 to $100 per year, and benefits include free admission to the facility you join plus discounted admission to other Bay Area museums and zoos through their affiliate programs. If you're a local, you can save big bucks and support these worthwhile organizations as well.

5. Pack a lunch. These are perfect for parks and natural areas, but even theme parks set space aside for do-it-yourself picnics. You can always buy treats to supplement what you bring.

GOOD TIMING

Most attractions with kid appeal are busiest when school is out. If you have preschool kids, try to tour crowded attractions (such as Alcatraz Island) on weekdays or in the off-season. If you want to go on a holiday, call ahead, as we list only regular operating hours. It's always a good idea to call ahead anyway, particularly if you're making a special trip. Attractions sometimes change their hours or close unexpectedly.

The weather also plays a role in good timing. San Francisco has an unusual weather pattern that catches many out-of-towners by surprise. Summertime can actually be one of the coolest seasons in the city, since that's when fog often blankets the bay. Anytime you set out for a day in the Bay Area, dress in layers. What can start out as a bright, sunny day can turn windy and cold before you can count to 10 goose bumps. The closer you get to the ocean, on the way seeing sights such as Ft. Funston, Ocean Beach, and the San Francisco Zoo, the better your chances of encountering fog.

OTHER SOURCES OF INFORMATION

The San Francisco Convention and Visitors Bureau (tel. 415/391-2000; www.onlyinsanfrancisco. com) has a visitor information center on the lower level of Hallidie Plaza (900 Market St., at Powell St.) in downtown San Francisco. Along with brochures and maps, you can pick up coupons and Muni transit passes. Hours are weekdays 9-5, weekends 9-3. There's also an official California Welcome Center office at San Francisco's Pier 39.

TRANSPORTATION

Even if you have a car, traffic and parking woes around crowded tourist attractions often make it unwise to drive. Mass transit alternatives include cable cars, buses, and streetcars. You can buy one-, three-, and seven-day adult passports for unlimited rides on Muni—including cable cars—for $11, $18, and $24, respectively (children ages 5-17 pay reduced prices anyway). Call 415/673-6864 for Muni information. You can also get connected to operators at just about any Bay Area transit office by calling 415/817-1717, the travelers information system.

MORE THINGS TO DO

Even a list of 68 activities can't cover everything there is to do with kids in the Bay Area. Watch for seasonal arts programs, such as the San Francisco Ethnic Dance

Festival (tel. 415/474–3914), which takes place each June and hosts dance troupes representing cultures around the globe, as well as special family concerts presented by the San Francisco Symphony (tel. 415/864–6000). The Greater Bay Area has a number of state parks ideal for a visit with kids, including Big Basin Redwood State Park (tel. 831/338–8860), with great hiking north of Santa Cruz; Tomales Bay State Park (tel. 415/669–1140), which has gentle beaches near Point Reyes National Seashore; Samuel P. Taylor State Park (tel. 415/488–9897), also in Marin County, where you can camp among the redwoods; Jack London State Historic Park (tel. 707/938–5216), in Sonoma County, where the famed adventure writer lived the last days of his life; and Ft. Ross State Historic Park (tel. 707/847–3286), on the Sonoma Coast, where you can see remnants of a 19th-century Russian outpost.

FINAL THOUGHTS

We'd love to hear yours: What did you and your kids think about the places we recommend? Have you found other places we should include? Send us your ideas via e-mail (c/o editors@fodors.com, specifying Around San Francisco with Kids on the subject line) or snail mail (c/o Around San Francisco with Kids, Fodor's Travel Publications, 1745 Broadway, New York, NY 10019). Meanwhile, have a great day around San Francisco with your kids!

ADVENTURE PLAYGROUND

With its multilayered, off-kilter scrap-wood forts, tire towers, and kid-painted wooden boats, Berkeley's Adventure Playground looks a bit like a children's hobo encampment. If your kids are the hands-on types, they'll love this dirt lot–cum–wonderland, where children design and build the play structures—or anything else they can imagine—themselves.

On the Berkeley waterfront, the playground rings with the sounds of hammers, handsaws, and squealing kids. Playhouses morph every day, with kids adding (and removing) ladders, walls, and entire stories to the many original structures. They can also design their own projects—a giant rocking chair, swords, sculptures—using the tools, wood, and recycled materials on-site. When they're done, they can paint their creation, or indeed take a paintbrush to anything else here, including the many (real) boats scattered about the yard—ideal for younger siblings not yet ready to wield a saw. Even those not into construction will find plenty to keep them busy: climb the giant tire tower, play pirate on a boat, attempt to walk a rope trapeze, or see how far they can get on the huge material-netting structure.

MAKE THE MOST OF YOUR TIME Needless to say, wear clothes
you don't care about, and be sure the kids have closed-toed shoes. The best time to visit—when there are enough tools to go around—is the afternoon of any dry day. Special programs happen throughout the summer, but most kids seem to prefer independent play here. Kids 7 and over can be dropped off for up to 3 hours for $6, a boon to parents with smaller children who'd rather play at the newly refurbished traditional playground next door. Especially with little ones, peek into the new Shorebird Park Nature Center here to see their aquarium and bird exhibits.

Kids (6 and over only) adore the one adult construction here: a 30-plus-foot zip line straight into a dirt pile.

The philosophy behind the playground is that by using real tools and materials to create on their own, children gain a sense of competence and confidence in their abilities. Anxious parents needn't worry that it's a free-for-all, though: throughout the day the large staff (mostly teenagers) and adult volunteers wander the yard looking for "Mister Dangerous"—unsteady structures, protruding nails, etc. In exchange for the tools and paints they need, kids turn in nails, wood chips, or pieces of trash they find around the playground—a remarkably effective system for keeping the place shipshape.

If you like this sight you may also like the Exploratorium (#47) and the Lawrence Hall of Science (#36).

KEEP IN MIND
Bringing an extra set of clothes for each kid might seem like a no-brainer. I didn't, though—what's a bit of dirt and paint?—but I hadn't factored in with the famous bay mud. If your kids are anything like mine and they're likely to head straight for the water, know that you'll be riding home with wet, putrid-smelling people in permanently stained clothes.

EATS FOR KIDS Picnic tables dot the play area next to the Adventure Playground, and there are plenty of pleasant spots along the marina. Bring supplies or stop for surprisingly good sandwiches, soup, or crustaceans at super low-key **Seabreeze Market and Deli** (598 University Ave., tel. 510/486–0802), just up the road. For a sit-down meal, head to bustling, riotously decorated **Juan's Place** (941 Carleton St., tel. 510/845–6904) for huge servings of traditional Mexican food and wine margaritas that go down easy.

ALCATRAZ ISLAND

67

The maximum-security prison on Alcatraz, closed in 1963, once held some of the nation's most incorrigible criminals—and though it's 1¼ miles and a 10-minute boat ride from Fisherman's Wharf, the 12-acre island still seems eerily isolated, its lighthouse tower often shrouded in mist. Over the past 150 years, the Rock has been a fortification, military prison, federal penitentiary, and site of an American Indian occupation. But since becoming a national park in 1973, Alcatraz has also become one of San Francisco's most popular tourist sites. Its history and gorgeous views are irresistible lures.

Hop one of the Alcatraz Cruises ferries, the only public transport to the island, and be sure to dress warmly and wear comfortable shoes—the island terrain is rocky and sometimes steep. Once here, you and your kids can peer into the tiny, spartan cells that once held the likes of Al Capone, Machine Gun Kelly, and Robert ("Birdman of Alcatraz") Stroud, and visit the grim "dark holes" where disobedient prisoners were left to languish by themselves in total darkness. Other sights include the shower room where prisoners were stripped

KEEP IN MIND Fairly often, especially in summer, former residents of Alcatraz—these days mostly children of prison workers and former guards—come to the Rock to regale visitors with their stories and sell their books in the gift shop. If you're lucky enough to meet one of these dwindling numbers, take advantage of it.

MAKE THE MOST OF YOUR TIME Don't even think about a last-minute trip to Alcatraz in summer, when cruises sell out up to two weeks in advance. Year-round you can skip the line and order tickets online; however, the Family Ticket—a great deal for four—can only be purchased by phone or at the Pier 33 ticket window. Check ahead of time about special Kidz Tourz, fun ranger-led programs designed for certain age groups. Pier 33 is within walking distance of some of the city's kid-friendliest places: Fisherman's Wharf and Pier 39. Older kids may still have plenty of energy after visiting the Rock; resist the urge to overdo.

Departures: Pier 33, Fisherman's Wharf

415/981-7625; www.nps. gov/alcatraz (park), www. alcatrazcruises.com (ferries)

Daytime tours $21.75 ages 12 and up, $13.75 children 5–11; evening tours $28.75 ages 18 and up, $27.75 ages 12–17, $17.25 children 5–11. Family ticket: 2 adults and 2 children ages 5–11, $66 (daytime tours only)

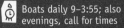
Boats daily 9–3:55; also evenings, call for times

5 and up

upon arrival at Alcatraz, the mess hall (complete with the last day's menu), and the exercise yard, where catwalks and guard towers loomed overhead. From the concrete bleachers, prisoners could glimpse the gleaming city across the bay and smell the coffee roasting in North Beach. Surprisingly, although Alcatraz could hold 450 prisoners, no more than 250 were ever incarcerated at a time, and barely a tenth of that number were here at the end.

Choose between taking a self-guided tour, using an audiocassette or pamphlet, or going with a ranger. School-age kids (and adults) are often riveted by the Cell House Audio Tour, which includes gravely voiced ex-inmates and stern guards describing their experiences. When it's open—usually September–January, depending on bird-nesting season—the Agave Trail, along the island's southern rim, makes for a great short hike. A visit to Alcatraz lasts 2–3 hours, but your kids will remember it for years to come.

If you like this sight you may also like Angel Island State Park (#66).

EATS FOR KIDS You can picnic around the Alcatraz dock but not beyond it—not an ideal arrangement—and there are no eateries on the island. Snacks are available on the ferry, and a small concessionaire at the Alcatraz Cruises landing on Pier 33 sells generic sandwiches and snacks. At the **Eagle Café** (Pier 39, tel. 415/433–3689), load up on big breakfasts and lunches in an old-time waterfront atmosphere. The bounty of the Ferry Building is a 15-minute walk away.

ANGEL ISLAND STATE PARK

Want to escape with your kids to an island park where the air is fresh, cars are banned, and grassy picnic areas, rocky coves, forested slopes, and 13 miles of hiking and biking trails await? Angel Island, the largest island in San Francisco Bay and a 25-minute ferry ride from Fisherman's Wharf, is both.

The fun begins on the Blue & Gold Fleet ferry ride across the bay (dress in layers, since the ride can get chilly). Once on the island, you can spread out a blanket or grab a picnic table at Ayala Cove, not far from the ferry dock, where there's plenty of grass, shade, and a small beach. Waters are cold and often rough and not meant for swimming, and there are no lifeguards. But lots of families hang out at the cove all day, tossing Frisbees or playing volleyball.

Alternatively, you can set off on a hiking or biking trip, best for kids ages 8 and up. The easiest route is the paved-and-gravel, mostly level, 5-mile Perimeter Road, which rings the

MAKE THE MOST OF YOUR TIME
Paying attention to the calendar—and your watch—can make a trip to Angel Island more pleasant. May and September tend to be less foggy and less congested than the summer months; if fog and wind are forecast, postpone your trip until a sunny day. Ferry and other services are limited from November to April. If you're bringing a bike, get to the ferry early; bike passage is limited and first-come, first-served. And unless you want to make an unexpected camping trip, allow plenty of time to catch the last ferry back to San Francisco.

entire island and offers 360-degree views of the bay. You can either bring your own bike or, from spring to fall, rent one near the dock ($10 per hour, $35 per day). If exercise doesn't appeal, a one-hour narrated tram tour ($9.50–$13.50), available March through November, covers much of the territory. Hikers can also climb to the top of the island on fairly narrow and steep dirt trails, recommended for kids 10 and older.

The island has nine hike-in campsites (tel. 800/444–7275; $15–$20). Sites 1–4 are best for small groups. Bring charcoal or a camp stove and prepare to haul equipment for 1 or 2 miles.

If you like this sight you may also like Alcatraz Island (#67).

KEEP IN MIND
Especially during summer, the events calendar at Angel Island is packed with special offerings that appeal to kids, from Civil War days and guided bike tours to Victorian Days, when costumed soldiers from the Spanish-American and Indian wars fire cannons and give other weapons demonstrations.

EATS FOR KIDS Considering the quality of the food available on the island, a picnic is the best way to go. The **Cove Café** (tel. 415/897–0715), near the island ferry dock, serves premade sandwiches, salads, and soups on a harbor-view deck; the outdoor Cantina & Oyster Bar, next door, caters to adults, offering bivalves and beer. The café and oyster bar are open daily May–October, with limited days March and November. For restaurants near Pier 41, see Fisherman's Wharf (#45) and Pier 39 (#19).

AÑO NUEVO STATE RESERVE

This reserve just off Highway 1, about 55 miles south of San Francisco, is home to one of California's great natural spectacles. Each winter, more than 4,000 massive Northern elephant seals come ashore to the beaches here to rest, mate, and give birth. Once nearly extinct, these protected marine mammals have staged a remarkable comeback, breeding successfully on Año Nuevo for more than 40 years.

The elephant seals spend much of their year out in the Pacific and in feeding grounds along British Columbia, Canada, to the north. The enormous males, weighing up to 3,000 pounds, are the first to return to Año Nuevo each December, battling each other for dominance in ferocious displays of raw power. The females, who weigh up to a ton, arrive around New Year's and give birth a few days later. Watching the newborn pups struggle to survive is a moving experience. Meanwhile, the adults mate again, usually in less than a month, and then head out to sea by mid-March, leaving the pups to learn to swim by themselves. By late April, the pups head north to Canada to feed. Older

KEEP IN MIND If a wet or windy day dampens your enthusiasm here, perhaps the best backup plan is watching the live feed of the seals on the screen at the visitors center.

MAKE THE MOST OF YOUR TIME Año Nuevo may be a state reserve, but this is no walk in the park during winter's mating and calving season, the best and most uncomfortable time to visit. Evaluate your kids' tolerance for discomfort and their maturity levels. Getting within 40 feet of elephant seals can be dangerous, so hold hands with young kids. Carry very small children in a backpack or front pack (no strollers). Dress for possible cold and windy weather and muddy terrain, and bring rain ponchos, since walks leave rain or shine and umbrellas aren't permitted. Allow up to 1½ hours to make the drive from San Francisco; late arrivals lose their reservations.

New Year's Creek Rd., Pescadero

650/879–0227 recording,
800/444–4445 reservations;
www.parks.ca.gov

 $6 per vehicle; guided
walks $5 per person
ages 4 and up

 Daily 8–sunset; guided walks
mid-Dec–Mar, daily 8:45–about 3

 6 and up

elephant seals return to molt from April to August, and yearling seals are often seen here in fall.

From mid-December to March the public is allowed to visit the breeding grounds only on naturalist-led guided walks, which cover 3 miles and last about 2½ hours. Reservations are essential and can be made starting in late October, up to eight weeks in advance. From April through November, free first-come, first-served permits to visit the elephant seal grounds are issued daily (8:30–3:30); allow 2–3 hours for the hike. During this mellow season, watching the inert seals is a lot "like watching paint dry," according to one naturalist. The reserve covers a wild, undeveloped coastal point of windswept dunes and rocky offshore islands, and in addition to the elephant seals, you can view a prolific assortment of sea lions, harbor seals, sea otters, offshore gray whales, and shorebirds.

If you like this sight you may also like Coyote Point Park and Museum (#49).

EATS FOR KIDS No food or beverages are sold at the reserve, but picnic tables are available. The nearest town, Pescadero, is the site of venerable **Duarte's Tavern** (202 Stage Rd., tel. 650/879–0464), known for its artichoke soup, seafood, and homemade pies, but kids can also get PB&Js. Also in Pescadero, cyclists pack the **Arcangeli Bakery** (287 Stage Rd., tel. 650/879–0147), inside the Country Deli, which makes fat deli sandwiches to order and has picnic tables out back.

AQUARIUM OF THE BAY

At Aquarium of the Bay, you and your children walk in clear acrylic tunnels to view an array of sharks, bat rays, eels, sturgeon, sea stars, and other creatures that dwell in San Francisco Bay. The concept is an intriguing one: People are, in effect, on the inside looking out into the tanks, while the marine life—swimming freely above and around the humans—are on the outside looking in.

Despite its prime location at Pier 39 (#19), the aquarium struggles to draw locals, many of whom view it primarily as a tourist attraction—or trap. It also faces tough competition from other area aquariums, such as the superlative Monterey Bay Aquarium and the newly renovated Steinhart Aquarium in Golden Gate Park (#41). If you're in the area and the high cost of admission doesn't put you off, this small aquarium merits a walk-through, especially for younger children.

MAKE THE MOST OF YOUR TIME The aquarium can be enjoyable and educational, but a family of four could easily spend $1 a minute or more for the experience. Factor in the well-stocked gift shop, which you enter when you "resurface." And that's not counting all the other ways to blow your budget on Pier 39. Save money by heading out of the neighborhood to eat—nearby North Beach and Chinatown have plenty of dining options—and take in the pier's free attraction: the barking sea lions. Head a few blocks west to Fisherman's Wharf (#45) and check out the Hyde Street Pier ships (free from the outside) on the way to the rolling lawns and boats at Ft. Mason.

Many families love what they see during their "dive into the bay" (actually an elevator descent, but dramatic license is allowed). Two 150-foot-long transparent tunnels usher you "into" a two-story tank that holds more than 700,000 gallons of water and 23,000 sea creatures. When you spot a shark swimming directly over your head—well, that's an experience not easily forgotten.

Hop on the slow-moving walkway that transports you through the tunnels. You can get off the walkway if you wish to stroll at your own pace or ask questions of the naturalist, if one is on duty. Figure 30–40 minutes to complete your "dive." (It's a bit awkward taking strollers on the moving walkway.) Later, kids get a chance to touch sea stars, sea urchins, and other creatures in a shallow tank.

If you like this sight you may also like the California Academy of Sciences (#57), the Oakland Zoo (#22), and the San Francisco Zoo (#11).

KEEP IN MIND

Though the Aquarium is appropriate for kids 3 and older the ideal range is 4 to 6; younger kids may not fully appreciate it (enough to justify the cost) and the older ones might be bored. If your kids are really into the ocean, consider saving the cost of admission to this site and driving down to the Monterey Bay Aquarium—it's also expensive, but you get far more bang for your buck.

EATS FOR KIDS If the Aquarium of the Bay gets you hungry for seafood, **Pier Market** (Pier 39, tel. 415/989–7437) dishes up mesquite-grilled fresh fish and good clam chowder. Nearby at Fisherman's Wharf, **Boudin Bakery** (160 Jefferson St., 415/928–1849) serves chowder in their famous sourdough bowls, along with hefty deli sandwiches; kids like the crab- and teddy bear–shape sourdough. For burgers, you can't beat **In-N-Out Burger** (333 Jefferson St., tel. 800/786–1000).

ARDENWOOD HISTORIC FARM

When was the last time your kids got to pump water, crank an old clothes wringer, or plant some crops? If the only hands-on activity they've gotten lately is hitting the button on the remote control, then head for the antidote for urban couch potatodom: Ardenwood Historic Farm. In southern Alameda County and part of the East Bay Regional Park District, Ardenwood is *the* place to introduce city children to life on a real working farm—a 19th-century farm at that. At this 200-acre complex, your kids—and you—can join in the pumping and cranking that were required to keep a farm going back in the Victorian age, and even help feed the livestock and plant, tend, and harvest the crops.

You can watch as costumed docents give farm-chore and craft-making demonstrations, such as horseshoe hammering, hay harvesting, lace-making, barrel-making, and biscuit baking. As on any farm, the activities change from season to season and even week to week; what you see and do in spring will be quite different from in the fall.

KEEP IN MIND
Ardenwood is a stop on the great Monarch butterfly migration circuit. During the winter, take a weekend train ride along the farm's eucalyptus stands and the ranger aboard will point out the clusters of hundreds of the fluttering orange creatures hanging in the trees.

MAKE THE MOST OF YOUR TIME
Special events at Ardenwood, such as fall's corn harvest and the Christmas programs are wonderful but crowded times to visit. For younger children, a picnic and visit to the animals may be enough, so head out during the week. The farm is out in the boonies, far from other attractions; It's best to plan to spend the day here. Needless to say, this isn't a rainy-day destination. To maintain the old-time atmosphere, Ardenwood doesn't allow anyone to bring modern play equipment, not even Frisbees, footballs, or soccer balls.

34600 Ardenwood Blvd., Fremont

 Mid-Nov–Apr and Apr–mid-Nov, Tu, W, and Sa $2 adults, $1 children 4–17; Apr–mid-Nov, Th, F, and Su $5 adults, $4 ages 4–17; special event admission varies

 T–Su 10–5 (last entrance 4); early Dec, Christmas tours

 510/796-0663 recording, 510/796-0199 voice

3 and up; house tours 6 and up

Ardenwood dates from the days following the 1849 Gold Rush, when a failed gold prospector named George Washington Patterson established a ranch here. Patterson's restored farmhouse and Victorian gardens are still on view, and you can take free tours of the house on a first-come, first-served basis. Most kids under 10 would find the tours a yawn, though they'd jump at the chance to take a horse-drawn hay wagon or horse-drawn train ride, both included in admission (except on Saturday, when they aren't available). Plenty of other farm animals are on hand, too, including sheep, goats, pigs, chickens, bunnies, turkeys, and cows.

Ardenwood hosts a variety of special events, which cost $1–$3 extra: old-fashioned July 4 and Christmas celebrations, summer and fall harvest festivals, concerts, and re-creations of Victorian-era social occasions.

If you like this sight you may also like the Presidio (#17) and Tilden Park (#6).

EATS FOR KIDS Ardenwood has nice picnic areas, and weekends May–October the **Farmyard Café** (tel. 510/797– 5621) here sells hot dogs, ice cream, and, for special events, barbecued foods. An open-air market sells fresh-picked organic fruits and vegetables just outside the farm. Nearby, Newark's Jarvis Avenue is lined with fast-food places.

BASIC BROWN BEAR FACTORY

As the owners of this factory put it, this is "a place where teddy bears are born." Since 1976, Merrilee and Eric Woods have been making teddy bears, and since 1985, they've let kids help in assembling, stuffing, and "bathing" them. Thousands of Bay Area kids have done just that, and it's become one of the top child-oriented factory tours in the country.

Here's how it works: Basic Brown Bear provides the pattern, material, stuffing, and instructions for a cuddly toy. Your child helps put it together, deciding how chubby or slender it will be and whether or not to add beans to liven up the polyester fiberfill. Staff and stuffing machine are there to assist, too. In fact, a staff member helps sew up the bear and groom it, and your youngster provides the final touch with a blow-dry "bath." All you have to do is pay for it.

The cost of the teddy bears depends on the size and complexity of the patterns, all of which are designed by Merrilee Woods and made right at the factory. There are more than 40 styles of bear to choose from. The least expensive (and simplest pattern), Baby Bear, stands 13

MAKE THE MOST OF YOUR TIME The bear factory—indeed the entire Cannery—is rarely crowded, so even on a weekend, this is a good choice. Before you head out, download a coupon for 10% off bear factory merchandise at www.thecannery. com. If your children are unimpressed with the bears or get through quickly, there's plenty to keep them occupied in this neighborhood, especially on sunny days. The cable cars turn around right outside; the ships of the Hyde Street Pier bob nearby; and Fisherman's Wharf and all its eye candy are short blocks away.

 Cannery, 2801 Leavenworth St.

 Free, bears $14–$150

Daily 10–6; tours daily 10–5

415/409–2806 or 866/522–2327;
www.basicbrownbear.com

2–10

inches high and costs $14. The biggest and most expensive, Big Fred, stands 3 feet tall and costs $150. A popular, moderately priced model, Gigi, costs $24. In addition, a full range of more than 70 outfits and accessories—dresses, tutus, jumpers, T-shirts, tuxedos, bridal outfits, vests, pants, surfer shirts, overalls, sleep shirts, sweaters, engineer outfits, and Nutcracker uniforms—are for sale.

The factory's free ½-hour drop-in tours demonstrate how the bears are designed, cut, and sewn. (These are geared to families or groups of eight or fewer; larger groups should call for reservations.) When all is said, done, and stuffed, your children will probably treasure these cuddly animals above others because they helped make them.

If you like this sight you may also like the Bay Area Discovery Museum (#61) and Children's Fairyland (#53).

KEEP IN MIND
Don't harbor any illusions about leaving the factory without purchasing a bear—the only children who wouldn't want one aren't the children you'd bring here in the first place. Take your new stuffed friends to the Cannery's courtyard, where umbrella-shaded tables are the perfect spot for a welcoming tea party.

EATS FOR KIDS Great, inexpensive made-to-order sandwiches are right downstairs at **Waterfront Bakery** (2801 Leavenworth St., tel. 415/775–2300), on the Cannery's street level. A block west at Ghirardelli Square, 1950s-style **Lori's Diner** (900 N. Point St., tel. 415/409–1950) serves big burgers, sandwiches, and sundaes; a 20% discount coupon is often available at www.lorisdiner.com. If it's Dungeness crab season (November–June), head down to the **food stands at Fisherman's Wharf**.

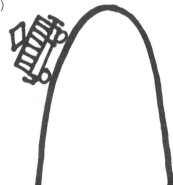

BAY AREA DISCOVERY MUSEUM

One of the state's top children's museums, the Bay Area Discovery Museum is housed in seven buildings that were once part of Ft. Baker, a former Army post currently morphing into an upscale resort. Now part of the Golden Gate National Recreation Area, the site has knockout views of the Golden Gate Bridge, since the museum rests virtually below its northern end. But for most kids, the views take a distant second place to the buzz of activities inside—all sorts of hands-on learning adventures, which to the uninitiated can bear a striking resemblance to playing.

Appropriately, the bay's natural wonders provide one realm of discovery. In the Bay Hall, your kids can crawl through a tunnel "beneath" the sea or fish aboard their own Discovery Boat. Live sea creatures swim in the Wave Workshop, where little kids can move stuffed versions around an "underwater" habitat and big kids can experiment with boats attached to cables in a water tank. Other attractions include art and ceramics studios for ages 5 and under and 6 and over. Toddlers have their own interactive discovery area—Tot Spot—

KEEP IN MIND The Discovery Museum's outdoor play areas, and some of its indoor studios, are divided strictly by age. Many kids are happy to spend their entire visit at Lookout Cove, which packs appeal for all ages; it's on the far end, but start your visit there.

MAKE THE MOST OF YOUR TIME The museum attracts far more kids in the under-5 crowd than bigger kids, but there's plenty to keep everyone occupied. Special programs cost additional fees and, while fun, are utterly unnecessary for a full experience. Even on weekends, the crowds really thin out after lunch when the toddler set heads home; plan an afternoon visit (especially weekdays during the school year) and your kids might have the run of the place. If the weather turns, head for the indoor Bay Model Visitor Center, in downtown Sausalito.

Ft. Baker, 557 E. McReynolds Rd., Sausalito

 $8 children ages 1 and up, $10 adults; programs $5–$8

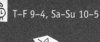 T–F 9–4, Sa–Su 10–5

415/339–3900; www.badm.org

0–8

where they can enter a storybook cave with adjustable lighting and an echo chamber, or sit on a waterbed and watch live fish above. Special exhibits change every few months. At the edge of the complex in the outdoor play area Lookout Cove, kids can clamber on a real fishing boat, use nuts and bolts to add panels to a gigantic model of the Golden Gate Bridge, and dig for treasure—including real pennies—among the ruins of a Spanish galleon. The landscaped nature area here includes gorgeous willow structures to wander through, giant frog sculptures, and huge reed nests with rock "eggs."

Half-hour weekday morning drop-in story-telling programs cater to toddlers and preschoolers. Drop-in Saturday art studio workshops, by contrast, are for ages 5 and up and happen about once per month. Other programs, which cost an additional $5–$8 per person, include sing-alongs and live theater performances.

If you like this sight you may also like the California Academy of Sciences (#57).

EATS FOR KIDS The museum's **Discovery Cafe** has outdoor seating and good food, much of it organic, appealing to both kids and parents. You can also picnic on the grounds. In downtown Sausalito, the legendary and creatively named **Hamburgers** (737 Bridgeway, tel. 415/332–9471) has, you guessed it, burgers and fries—plus fish-and-chips, hot dogs, and ice cream. Sit inside, where it's cramped, or get your food to go. Stop for good coffee and pastries at **Northpoint Coffee Company** (1250 Bridgeway, tel. 415/ 331–0777), with a glorious back deck overlooking the water.

BAY CRUISES

A big part of the San Francisco Bay experience is getting out on the water, and kids are often among the most enthusiastic boat riders. Two of the most popular trips go to Alcatraz Island and Angel Island State Park (#67 and #66), and, May–October, you can even combine the two in a one-day extravaganza offered by the Blue & Gold Fleet. But if you just want a boat trip without touring islands on the other end or if your timing isn't right for an Alcatraz or Angel Island trip, there's another good option: a one-hour bay cruise. Take your pick between the Blue & Gold Fleet, operating from Pier 39's west marina, and the Red & White Fleet, leaving from Pier 43½, at Fisherman's Wharf. The trips are similar, and the costs are the same.

The narrated cruises hit the bay highlights, providing unobstructed views from the water and offering a little history along the way. Leaving the wharf area, you'll get nice perspectives of the San Francisco waterfront and the skyline beyond, including landmarks such as Coit Tower (*see* listings for many of these sights) and the Transamerica Pyramid.

MAKE THE MOST OF YOUR TIME If you don't want to pay
cruise boat prices, but you still want to get out on the water, ride a ferryboat instead. There's
no narration, but the scenery's just as good. Blue & Gold Fleet runs ferries to Oakland's Jack
London Square in the East Bay and to Sausalito and Tiburon in Marin, among other destinations. The areas around the landings at Oakland, Sausalito, and Tiburon all offer plenty
of dining and ambling options, along with waterfront scenery and places to run. Golden
Gate Ferry (tel. 415/923–2000), meanwhile, runs ferryboats to Sausalito and Larkspur, also
in Marin; Larkspur's landing is a walk from town.

Departures from Piers 39 and 43½

 $21 adults, $17–$18 youths 12–18, $13–$14 children 5–11

 Daily with varying times

Blue & Gold: 415/773-1188 recording, 415/705-5555 tickets, www.blueandgoldfleet.com; Red & White: 415/447-0597, www.redandwhite.com

5 and up

Boats pass by the southern side of Alcatraz, then head west past Presidio National Park and Ft. Point on the way toward the Golden Gate Bridge. For many kids, the big thrill of the cruise is passing beneath the bridge, whose towers rise nearly 750 feet in the air. The boats then turn back east, providing good views of the Marin Headlands and the Mediterranean-style village of Sausalito to the north. In the last few minutes you'll circle around Angel Island and then head back south past Alcatraz to the docks.

Even on the bay, which is usually placid compared to the ocean, you might want to take seasickness precautions for your children (check with your pediatrician about appropriate medications). Also remember that it can get very cold and windy on the water, even on a sunny day, so dress in layers.

If you like this experience you may also like the Hyde Street Pier (#39).

EATS FOR KIDS Cruise boats have small **snack bars** aboard, selling drinks, chips, and the like, but don't count on them for real meals. Good eateries near the pier include the **Eagle Café** (Pier 39, tel. 415/433–3689) and **Alioto's** (8 Fisherman's Wharf, tel. 415/673–0183).

KEEP IN MIND If the weather is fine, grab seats on the upper deck. Outside small children are less likely to be hushed by passengers straining to hear the narration, and everyone has a front-row seat for all the sights.

BAY MODEL VISITOR CENTER

Everyone knows San Francisco is the City by the Bay, but the size and geography of the bay—as well as other nearby waterways—can be confusing even for longtime residents. Walking through this 1½-acre, hydraulic, three-dimensional scale model of the bay, housed inside a onetime shipbuilding facility, helps your family make sense of all that water.

Operated by the U.S. Army Corps of Engineers, the Bay Model looks like a cross between a science experiment and a huge work of modern art. Don't expect bells and whistles, though; this is a scientific facility, built in the 1950s to test possible ways of damming the bay to store fresh water. No dams were built, but the model now enables scientists and engineers to study the bay's water flow and tidal patterns and to measure the effects of both natural phenomena (such as drought and floods) and human activities on local waters. It's all intended to help the corps protect wetlands, control flooding, manage natural disasters, and keep waterways navigable.

KEEP IN MIND It's easy to walk around the entire model and still have little idea what the whole thing is for. This is one of those places where asking questions pays big dividends, so even if you don't have the 10-person minimum for a tour, pick the ranger's brain—their knowledge of the bay is superseded only by their enthusiasm.

MAKE THE MOST OF YOUR TIME Tours of the Bay Model are self-guided, so pick up a map when you enter. If you have a minimum of 10 people in your group, you can reserve a ranger-led tour geared toward the ages of the kids and your particular interests. Audiotape tours are available for $3, though younger kids might find these boring. Allow about 1½ hours for any tour, though a walk through can be done in 30 minutes. Since this is a relatively short stop, have a plan for afterward (or a backup plan in case the kids are less than riveted). Downtown Sausalito, just down the street, has tons of fun shopping and dining.

2100 Bridgeway, Sausalito

415/332–3870 recording, 415/332–3871 voice; www.spn.usace.army.mil/bmvc

 Free

Memorial Day–Labor Day, T–F 9–4, Sa–Su 10–5; early Sept–late May, T–Sa 9–4

8 and up

For young visitors (age 9 and up is best), hands-on educational exhibits and videos depict the bay's natural history, wildlife, geology, and fishing industry. You and your children can walk on ramps to get an overview of just how big the bay is; kids as young as 6 enjoy recognizing landmarks like the Golden Gate Bridge (#42), Alcatraz (#67), and San Francisco International Airport. The model comprises nearly 300 12-foot by 12-foot, 5-ton slabs of concrete, representing 343 square miles of bay, river, ocean, and land, all reproduced to scale.

Just before the exit, you'll pass through the Marinship exhibit, which chronicles the time when 20,000 workers—including many women—put the final touches on liberty ships and tankers here during World War II. Watch video testimonials of a variety of folks who worked here during that heady time, see models of the vehicles they built, and stand toe to toe with mannequins in full military uniform.

If you like this sight you may also like the Coyote Point Park and Museum (#49).

EATS FOR KIDS You can picnic at tables on the waterfront near the Bay Model or on one of the benches in the grassy park areas between Bridgeway and the bay, near the ferry terminal. **Scoma's** (588 Bridgeway, tel. 415/332–9551) has bay views, decent seafood, and a children's menu. Also on Bridgeway is **Hamburgers** (737 Bridgeway, tel. 415/332–9471), a mostly take-out eatery. For more formal meals, try the **Cat 'N' Fiddle** (303 Johnson St., tel. 415/332–4912), across from the Sausalito Yacht Harbor, where the seafood comes with water views.

CABLE CAR MUSEUM

When a cable car comes by—bells clanging, brakes screeching, cables humming—everybody, whether kid or grown-up, turns to watch. Cable cars are the only National Historic Landmarks that *move*. But what is it that makes these Victorian-age conveyances go (without engines!) and keeps them on track—up and down some of the city's steepest hills? You'll find out at the Cable Car Museum.

Of course, first you have to get here, and the only way to go is by cable car. Well, you could drive, but what fun would that be? And parking is nearly impossible to find anyway. Hop on the Powell-Mason Line or the Powell-Hyde Line either downtown or in the Fisherman's Wharf area. Then ask the conductor to call out the Cable Car Museum, situated in the 1907 redbrick cable car barn and powerhouse at the corner of Washington and Mason streets, near Chinatown. The cable car ride may cost $5 per person (under 5 free), but with free admission to the museum, you're still ahead of the game.

MAKE THE MOST OF YOUR TIME Cable cars are often crowded, and long lines form at the turnarounds. But you don't have to board at turnarounds; cars stop every other block or so (look for maroon-and-white signs). Make sure small children are safely inside, holding on, before the car moves. The Powell–Hyde line, with its steep ride to Fisherman's Wharf, is the most dramatic and the most crowded, and well worth it. The city's Indian summer of September and October is the best time to ride the cars: warm, clear, and less crowded than summer. If the kids are serious cable car fans, consider buying an all-day pass for $10. Buy tickets or passes from the conductor onboard, cash only.

1201 Mason St., Nob Hill, Russian Hill

415/474–1887;
www.cablecarmuseum.com

 Free

 Apr–Sept, daily 10–6; Oct–Mar, daily 10–5

3 and up

Once inside on a self-guided tour, you'll learn the ingenious secrets of cable power, developed more than 125 years ago by Andrew Hallidie, an engineer and immigrant from Scotland, who tested the first cable car on nearby Clay Street. It's simple, really: Four sets of cables make a continuous 9½-mph circuit beneath city streets; the cars, which grip the cables, automatically travel along with them. The cable system—on view on the lower level here—is run by huge revolving wheels that pull and steer the cables as they enter and leave the powerhouse. (You can hear the whirring sounds as soon as you come in.) Up on the mezzanine, a museum displays three antique model cable cars, including one from the Clay Street Railroad, the first cable car company. You'll also find plenty of old photographs, a 16-minute film showing how cable cars operate, and a museum shop.

If you like this sight you may also like the California State Railroad Museum (#56).

KEEP IN MIND For kids who can't get enough of big, shiny trains, combine a cable-car day with a ride on the city's other signature transportation, the vintage trolleys of the F-line. If you ride the cable car to Fisherman's Wharf, you can transfer to the F-line and ride it to the Ferry Building or on to the cable-car turnaround at Powell and Market streets.

EATS FOR KIDS Dining around the museum is nigh nonexistent. In North Beach, aromatic, salami-hung **Molinari Delicatessen** (373 Columbus Ave., tel. 415/421–2337) serves made-to-order sandwiches big enough for two. Take them down Columbus to Washington Square Park for a picnic and excellent urban people watching. The **Pot Sticker** (150 Waverly Pl., tel. 415/397–9985) has good, inexpensive Chinese food, such as pan-fried dumplings filled with meat or vegetables.

CALIFORNIA ACADEMY OF SCIENCES

57

Completely renovated beginning in 2005 and scheduled to reopen in fall 2008, the new academy is a huge complex in the heart of Golden Gate Park that actually contains three family attractions in one—a natural history museum, aquarium, and planetarium providing windows into the earth, ocean, and space. Start with the Steinhart Aquarium, included in museum admission, the biggest part of the complex. Here kids can walk across a glass bridge and wonder at the 25-foot-deep live coral tank—the world's deepest—and eyeball black-tip sharks, zebra sharks, and sea turtles. In the four-story Rainforests of the World exhibit, see vegetarian piranhas and giant catfish in the massive tank; check out giant anacondas, poison dart frogs, and flying lizards; and walk among free-flying tropical birds. The academy's beloved alligators and snapping turtles inhabit the Swamp, and nine African penguins frolic in the aquarium's Africa Hall. Young children, especially, like to get their hands wet at the Touch Tidepool, where they can pick up sea stars, anemones, and slimy sea cucumbers.

KEEP IN MIND A terrific add-on to a visit to the academy is right across the street: head to the de Young Museum (50 Hagiwara Tea Garden Dr., 415/750–3600) and up the elevator to the ninth-story observation floor. The floor-to-ceiling windows give views across the park (including over the academy) into the distance.

MAKE THE MOST OF YOUR TIME You can save money on admission here by riding public transit to Golden Gate Park; show a valid ticket, transfer, or monthly pass and get $2.50 off general admission to the museum. (The Muni No. 44 O'Shaughnessy bus goes directly to the front entrance.) The museum is free to all on the first Wednesday of each month, and it also has a variety of "neighborhood free days" each fall, for San Francisco residents only; call 415/750–7144 for more information. Call ahead for feeding times for the penguins, sharks, and giant snakes. If the weather is fine, make a visit to the Cal Academy part of a day in the park.

55 Concourse Dr., near 8th Ave. and Fulton St., Golden Gate Park

 $10 adults, $6.50 youths 12–17 and students, $2 children 4–11; planetarium $2.50 adults, $1.25 children 6–17; 1st W of mth free

 Daily 10–5; 3rd Th until 9 PM

415/750–7145 recording, 415/221–5100 voice, 415/750–7127 planetarium; www.calacademy.org

2 and up; planetarium 6 and up

At the Kimball Natural History Museum, one of the world's 10 largest, your kids will come face to face with a skeleton of a Tyrannosaurus rex and other dinosaur fossils. Your kids can touch an elephant skin at the Africa Experience, and kids 5 and under can head to the Africa Playspace to try on costumes and watch puppet shows.

One of the museum's most striking features is its "living roof," that hilly, lumpy part up top that's covered with living plants. Wildflowers shoot up from a grass carpet (held in place by rocks, pebbles, and coconut fiber), which helps the museum minimize its ecological footprint. One of those lumps on the roof covers the 90-foot dome of the Morrison Planetarium, where you can watch live coverage of NASA space missions and eclipses, view computer animation and science shows, and see the usual star shows; all these cost extra.

If you like this sight you may also like the Lawrence Hall of Science (#36).

EATS FOR KIDS The museum's **cafeteria** is open until an hour before closing. Pick up one of the finest gourmet pizzas around at **Arizmendi Bakery** (1331 9th Ave., tel. 415/566–3117), a breezy co-op with a tiny seating area and pies to go. **Park Chow** (1240 9th Ave., tel. 415/665–9912) is a bustling place with both indoor and outdoor tables and an eclectic menu ranging from spaghetti and little pizzas to Asian-style noodles. This one's best suited for kids 10 and up, or, if younger, with sophisticated tastes.

The city of Sacramento (about 90 miles east of San Francisco via I–80) gave birth to the idea for the first transcontinental railroad. So it's a fitting setting for this outstanding facility, the largest interpretive railroad museum in North America. In fact, the 19th century is very much alive at the museum, part of Old Sacramento State Historic Park—a 28-acre restored Gold Rush–era district with Victorian buildings, wooden boardwalks, gas lamps, and cobbled streets—lying along the Sacramento River. Budding engineers love to clamber aboard the museum's beautifully restored historic train cars. Films, slide shows, and exhibits, mainly of interest to older kids, recount the role the trains played in history. Volunteers, many ex-railway workers, are on hand to answer questions.

The oldest locomotive in the collection, the 1863 Southern Pacific *No. 1 C.P. Huntington,* was used in building the transcontinental railroad. But that one is dwarfed by an enormous 1944 Southern Pacific steam locomotive, one of the largest ever. It's 125 feet long and weighs more than a million pounds. Don't miss a walk through the 1929 Canadian National

MAKE THE MOST OF YOUR TIME You could easily spend the rest of a day exploring Old Sacramento State Historic Park (tel. 916/442–7644). Your family can take a horse-drawn carriage ride or paddle-wheeler cruise along the river, or, on weekends April–September, ride along the river on a steam train: the Sacramento Southern Railroad ($8 adults, $3 children 6–17). There's also an old schoolhouse to tour, a vintage theater, a Wells Fargo museum, and the Discovery Museum (101 I St., tel. 916/264–7057), a hands-on science and history facility.

2nd and I Sts., Sacramento

 $8 adults, $3 ages 6–17

 Daily 10–5

916/445–6645;
www.californiastaterailroadmuseum.org

4 and up

Railways sleeper the *St. Hyacinthe,* in which special light, sound, and rocking-motion effects create the illusion of clattering down the rails during the night. (Some little ones get a bit freaked out in this one.)

An entire gallery is dedicated to *Small Wonders: The Magic of Toy Trains*, one of the biggest model-train displays around, with more than 7,000 toy trains traveling through a finely detailed miniature landscape. Even the littlest tots get a kick out of discovering animals, fire trucks, and flashing wigwags among the display. Tickets to the museum also include admission to the nearby reconstructed Central Pacific Passenger Station (930 Front St.), a circa-1870 station with separate waiting rooms for ladies and children and a refreshment stand selling sarsaparilla.

If you like this sight you may also like the Hiller Aviation Museum (#40).

EATS FOR KIDS For 1870s-era atmosphere and contemporary food, head for the **Silver Palace Restaurant** (920 Front St., tel. 916/448–0151), in the Central Pacific Railroad Passenger Station. Aboard the vintage paddle wheeler *Delta King,* the **Pilothouse Restaurant** (1000 Front St., tel. 916/441–4440) serves seafood and nouvelle cuisine.

KEEP IN MIND
The drive up to Sacramento can be a long trip for kids, especially if you hit traffic. Try to arrive around 10 in the morning and on a summer weekend when the train ride is operating.

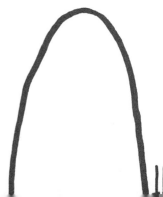

CARTOON ART MUSEUM

Old toons never die. They just go to the Cartoon Art Museum. This is the place where Bill Watterson's classic comic duo, Calvin and Hobbes, live on. So do old-timers Krazy Kat and the Green Lantern. You'll also find the familiar figures of Snoopy, Charlie Brown, Batman, Bugs Bunny, and Dennis the Menace. Here, cartoons are treated with all the reverence usually accorded other types of art. Founded in 1984, it's the only museum on the West Coast that's dedicated to preserving, collecting, and exhibiting original cartoon art in all its forms. Though cartoon-loving kids enjoy it, the museum is primarily designed for grown-up connoisseurs; if your children aren't serious fans, skip this one.

The museum's 12,000-piece permanent collection displays works from 1730 (a political cartoon by William Hogarth, an English artist considered the father of modern caricature) to 1895 (the Yellow Kid, the first successful newspaper comic strip character) to modern day ("Peanuts," "Doonesbury," "Zippy the Pinhead" strips). Included in the collection, besides comic strips, are editorial cartoons, comic books (including underground and avant-garde),

KEEP IN MIND The difference between a fantastic visit to the Cartoon Art Museum and a mediocre one is all in the timing. Temporary exhibits range political—how the U.S. is represented in international comics, for example—to kid friendly, such as a Charles M. Schulz retrospective. Consult the museum's online calendar.

MAKE THE MOST OF YOUR TIME Some cartoons on display (especially in special exhibitions) may be R- or X-rated. If this is a concern, you may want to do a little advance scouting or call the museum first before bringing your kids and being unpleasantly surprised. And if even your comic-book fans get glossy-eyed viewing the framed pages, be prepared to cut your visit short and switch gears. The Yerba Buena area has tons of options, from the fountain-studded Yerba Buena Gardens—great for romping—with its gorgeous antique carousel and the more hands-on cultural exhibits at the Museum for the African Diaspora to the video arcade and movies at the Metreon.

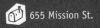 655 Mission St.

 415/227-8666; www.cartoonart.org

 $6 adults, $4 students, $2 children 6–12; classes $5

T–Su 11–5

6 and up

magazines, advertisements, newspapers, sculptures, and animation drawings. Among the latter, look for animation cels from Bugs Bunny cartoons, Pink Panther productions, and Peanuts TV shows as well as Disney studio drawings from such films as *Pinocchio, Fantasia, Snow White, Peter Pan,* and *101 Dalmatians.* Your kids may also enjoy discovering old-time comic strip artists like Jimmy Hatlo ("They'll Do It Every Time") and Harold Foster ("Prince Valiant").

At the museum's Children's Gallery, kids ages 6–14 can take Saturday cartooning classes. Given by a professional cartoonist, they teach kids how to draw some of their favorite cartoon characters as well as how to create their own strips. Classes last two hours and cost $5, with materials included; call the museum for dates. Maybe someday your own child's work will adorn these same walls.

If you like this sight you may also like the Charles M. Schulz Museum in Santa Rosa (2301 Hardies Lane, tel. 707/579-4452).

EATS FOR KIDS Just up the street, conveniently tucked alongside the nearest public parking garage, a branch of **Mels Drive-In** (801 Mission St., tel. 415/227–0793) serves up big, juicy burgers and tasty fountain drinks with a colorful '50s-diner theme. Kids' meals are served in cardboard classic cars. For other family-friendly spots in the immediate area, stop by the **Metreon** (101 4th St.) shopping complex. Also see the San Francisco Museum of Modern Art and Yerba Buena Gardens; the latter is a superlative spot for picnics, so grab your fare to take out.

CHABOT SPACE & SCIENCE CENTER

Kids can travel to space through hands-on exhibits, stargazing, and movies at this $70 million, state-of-the-art facility in sprawling, redwood-dotted Joaquin Miller Park, high in the Oakland Hills. At 1,540 feet in elevation, the observatory provides access to the country's largest telescope that's regularly open to the public—a 36-inch reflector. (Historic 8-inch and 20-inch refractors are still on hand, too.)

General admission gives you access to a variety of permanent and temporary, hands-on exhibits focusing on astronomy and the interrelationships of all sciences and technology. Make a beeline for One Giant Leap: A Moon Odyssey, which spans all three floors. Around a 30-plus-foot model of the Saturn 5 rocket, you can climb aboard a claustrophobic re-creation of the Mercury capsule, use a simulator to land a lunar module, and see spacesuits worn by real astronauts and cosmonauts. In Solar Go Round—fun for all but best for kids 9–12—you get to create volcanoes and windswept landscapes, play with clouds and supercooled icy bodies, and touch a meteorite; for little kids there's even a puzzle or two.

MAKE THE MOST OF YOUR TIME
You can easily run up a big tab here. If you add a megadome movie to regular admission, it's $21 for an adult, $17 for a student, and $16 for a child; if you add a special planetarium show as well, it's $29, $24, and $23. Unless your kids have a burning passion for one of the subjects covered in these extras, stick with the exhibits and the planetarium show that's included in regular admission. Also: The center is almost never crowded, and it's a good rainy-day option, unless you plan to take advantage of the observatory.

10902 Skyline Blvd., Oakland

510/336-7300, 510/336-7373
box office; www.chabotspace.org

 $13 adults, $10 students
with ID, $9 children 3–12;
some planetarium shows
and theater extra

 July–Aug T–Th 10–5, F–Sa 10–10, Su
11–5; mid-Sept–June W–Th 10–5, F–Sa
10–10, Su 11–5; closed 2 wks in Sept

6 and up

Among the complex ideas in Destination Universe are rubbing plates with cosmic designs, a crawl-through black hole, and one very cool giant kaleidoscope. The changing, hands-on exhibits upstairs are often worth a stop; in these kids got to do things like "rearrange" the earth's landscape, showing how nothing ever stays the same, or step inside a gigantic bat head to experience echolocation. If you have little ones in tow, when they start to get antsy with the big exhibits, head for the all-touch Discovery Lab. Here kids can build rockets, dress up like a shuttle astronaut, view insects under microscopes, build with Legos, or play games at computer stations. Admission also includes a show in the 240-seat planetarium, one of the most advanced in the world.

If you like this sight you may also like the California Academy of Sciences (#57), the Exploratorium (#47), and the Lawrence Hall of Science (#36).

KEEP IN MIND

With its multifaceted approach to various disciplines, this facility has struggled to attract visitors. While it's well worth a visit, Chabot should be a distant third behind the Exploratorium and the California Academy of Sciences on your to-do list, especially with kids under 10. Every evening you can come out for free stargazing through the center's telescopes.

EATS FOR KIDS Be aware that the space center's ultracasual, self-serve **Celestial Café** is only open weekends; it offers sandwiches (roast beef, turkey, PB&J) as well as fresh fruit and drinks. There are both indoor and outdoor tables, the latter on a terrace with nice views looking down over Oakland. Joaquin Miller Park has plenty of picnic space, and there's a branch of **Round Table Pizza** (2854 Mountain Blvd., tel. 510/336–3333) down the hill a bit from the space center. The upscale Montclair neighborhood, one exit north on Highway 13, has a lively shopping area along Park Boulevard with kid-friendly dining options.

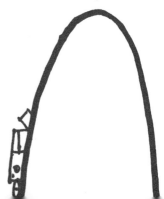

CHILDREN'S FAIRYLAND

This 10-acre storybook theme park, the first of its kind in the country, has another possible claim to fame: Walt Disney himself visited here a few years before opening Disneyland in 1955, and it may have helped inspire the idea for the Magic Kingdom. One thing's certain: Children's Fairyland has enchanted local children for more than a half century. You won't find any teens zooming by on daredevil rides or any high-tech gadgets catering to the over-10 set here. At this clean, low-key theme park, the stage is set entirely for young kids.

A Magic Key, purchased for a one-time fee, unlocks "talking storybooks," bringing more than 30 colorful nursery rhyme and fairy-tale sets to old-fashioned, gravelly voiced life. Tots can gaze through the window of Geppetto's workshop, pass through Alice in Wonderland's tunnel, enter the mouth of Willie the Whale, visit Peter Rabbit's Village, and view the Three Billy Goats Gruff—complete with live goats. Puppet shows, storytelling, and a little animal corral with donkeys, rabbits, ponies, and sheep—kids can pet them from 1 to 2 on weekends—provide more entertainment for the littlest visitors. So do a few gentle mini-rides—two

KEEP IN MIND A cool oddity, even in this multicultural city, is Gondola Servizio (tel. 866/737–8494), which offers authentic Venetian gondola rides on Lake Merritt. Even if you don't want to reserve a ride—they start at $45 per half hour—it's fun to see the straw-hatted gondolier plying the lake's waters.

MAKE THE MOST OF YOUR TIME Visiting after lunch is best for kids over 4—most of the tots have gone home to nap, leaving fewer strollers and little ones to maneuver around. After visiting Children's Fairyland, you can explore other parts of 120-acre Lakeside Park, on pretty Lake Merritt. A man-made saltwater lake—a rare phenomenon in the middle of a city—Lake Merritt was the country's first state game refuge, and there's still a waterfowl refuge here. Playgrounds, gardens, picnic spots, a natural science center, a bandstand, and waterfowl-feeding areas await at various points around the park.

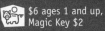
carousels, a tiny Ferris wheel, and a trolley—all of which are included in the unlimited-ride admission price. All this may prove too tame for kids over 3. In that case, skip the fairy-tale stuff and head straight for the themed climb-on-and-run-through areas. Play Island, based on the tale of the Swiss Family Robinson, is like a multilevel tree house complete with bridges and tropical-style huts. On the Jolly Roger Pirate Ship, kids can scale a rope sail to the crow's nest—fun even if they don't know the story of Peter Pan. Old West Junction is an entire town—for pint-size people—including a jail, a bank, and slides down from the second stories.

The park hosts a number of special events throughout the year, including a Halloween Jack-O-Lantern Jamboree and Winter Wonderland. There are also performing arts summer camps for kids 5–11, roles for kids 8–10 in Fairyland plays (audition required), and overnight family campouts in summer.

If you like this site, you may also like the Bay Area Discovery Museum (#61).

EATS FOR KIDS Fairyland's **Johnny Appleseed Café** serves reasonably priced hot dogs, burgers, fruit, and drinks in a casual garden setting, and the park has picnic areas, too. You can also bring your own food to picnic along the banks of Lake Merritt, where plenty of grass and shade trees invite spreading out a blanket (watch out for those geese, though). Italian fare is served at lively **Zza's Trattoria** (552 Grand Ave., tel. 510/839–9124), an informal restaurant near the lake. **Zachary's Chicago Pizza** (5801 College Ave., tel. 510/655–6385) has some of the area's best deep-dish pies.

CHINA BEACH

ocket-size China Beach isn't a snap to find, but for those who seek it out, a reward awaits: It's a sheltered, rarely crowded stretch of sand that offers jaw-dropping views of the Golden Gate Bridge and the Marin Headlands, and kids enjoy watching massive container ships pass through the Golden Gate. Named for a group of poor Chinese fishermen who lived beside the beach during the Gold Rush era and now tucked below the palatial homes of the tony Seacliff area in the Richmond District, China Beach is a 600-foot sandy strip that's shielded by cliffs on either side.

The Golden Gate's unpredictable tides and undertows make swimming here a risky proposition, but for toe-dipping and a romp in the sand, this is one of the best spots in town. The water tends to be pretty chilly, hovering around the 60s in summer, and, like all San Francisco beaches, it can get socked in by summer fog. Though small compared to other beaches, China Beach still has room to toss a Frisbee around, and you'll be treated to views that match the million-dollar price tags of the homes perched above. You might

MAKE THE MOST OF YOUR TIME From the parking lot above,

it's 92 steps down to the beach, something to keep in mind when you're towing beach gear, a cooler, barbeque supplies—and small children. Of course the beach is most pleasant on still, sunny days, but if your kids are real sand crabs and bundled in warm clothing, you can easily spend the entire day here. If the weather drives you away, though, head up to Clement Street; with its bounty of restaurants, cafés, and bakeries—not to mention the treasure trove that is Green Apple Books (506 Clement St., tel. 415/387–2272)—you'll surely find shelter.

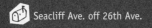

even spot a marine mammal or two—perhaps a sea lion, dolphins, or a daredevil surfer (the human variety).

The facilities are good here, too (it's run by the National Park Service). You'll find free changing rooms, showers, rest rooms, barbecue pits, picnic tables, and—if lying on sand isn't your thing—an enclosed sundeck for stretching out on your beach towel. Those with tots can push strollers all the way to the beach; look for the ramp on the left side. Small though it is, China Beach manages to pack a lot in.

If you like this sight you may also like Angel Island State Park (#66), Lake Merced (#37), and Ocean Beach (#21).

KEEP IN MIND
At low tide, a special adventure opens up: you can walk all the way from China Beach to Baker Beach, finding crabs, starfish, and sea snails in the tide pools along the way. Be aware that Baker Beach is a favorite nude sunbathing spot, and head back before the tide does.

EATS FOR KIDS There are no restaurants right next to China Beach, so the handiest thing to do is pack a picnic lunch or snacks or use the beach's barbecue facilities. Friendly **A K Meats** (2346 Clement St., tel. 415/933–6328) is a butcher shop serving up fresh, tasty deli sandwiches and house-made soup; half sandwiches are plenty for most kids.

CHINATOWN

Chinatown can be magical for kids: Neon signs, pagoda roofs, dragon-entwined lampposts, and shops packed with strange-looking herbs all add to its exotic allure. One of the largest Chinese communities outside Asia, it's a tightly packed, colorful 24-block jumble of restaurants, teahouses, temples, souvenir shops, and markets.

The only way to see the area is on foot. Start at the green-tiled, dragon-topped Chinatown Gate (Bush St. and Grant Ave.). It's much like entering a city within a city. Walk north up Grant Avenue—Chinatown's main thoroughfare—lined with bazaars, restaurants, and curio shops. Some items, often piled high in baskets on the sidewalk—conveniently at kid height—are quite inexpensive. But don't limit yourself to Grant. To the west, Stockton Street (where Chinese shop for produce and fresh fish) has a more authentic feel, as do many small alleyways near by. Stockton is the place to see live animals—sharks, frog, game birds—for sale in tanks and cages, though this can upset the tenderhearted. The Chinese Six Companies Building (843 Stockton St.), with curved roof tiles and pagoda top, should catch your

KEEP IN MIND If you drive to Chinatown—a huge hassle—dump your car as soon as possible; there are lots at the south end (Portsmouth Square Garage, enter on Kearny St.) and the north end (North Beach Parking Garage, enter on Vallejo). And keep in mind that Chinatown is still largely cash only.

MAKE THE MOST OF YOUR TIME One of the most colorful times to visit Chinatown is during the Chinese New Year, generally in late February or early March. The Chinese New Year Parade (tel. 415/982–3000), held on a Saturday evening, is one of few remaining illuminated night parades. The Chinatown Street Fair, the same weekend, features kite making, lion dancing, and calligraphy. Other than Chinese New Year, the best time to visit is on a sunny Saturday, when all the shops and restaurants are open and the streets bustle with locals running errands.

Bounded by Columbus Ave. and
Bush, Kearny, Vallejo, and Powell Sts.

 Free

Daily 24 hrs

415/982–6306;
www.sanfranciscochinatown.com

5 and up

kids' eyes. Along narrow side streets like Waverly Place, Spofford Lane, and Ross Alley, you can hear the click of mah-jongg tiles, the whir of sewing machines, and the clinking of teacups. At the Golden Gate Fortune Cookie Factory (56 Ross Alley, tel. 415/781–3956), your kids can discover how fortunes get inside.

The Tien Hou Temple (125 Waverly Pl.) is the oldest Buddhist temple in the United States; climb to the third floor, where the air is redolent of incense and the decor features red-and-gold lanterns and carved wooden deities; only bring kids old enough to keep respectfully quiet and not touch anything. The most fun for kids may be walking over Kearny via the footbridge to Portsmouth Square, site of an early settlement, where elders greet the morning with tai chi exercises. Men then play cards and a Chinese version of chess, while grandmothers watch children on the playground.

If you like this sight you may also like Japantown (#38) and the Italian quarter of North Beach.

EATS FOR KIDS For a snack, get almond cookies, moon cakes, or steamed pork buns at one of the many Chinese bakeries (Golden Gate Bakery at 1029 Grant is the best), or buy fortune cookies. For lunch, try dim sum (filled dumplings and other small dishes, usually chosen from carts wheeled from table to table). **Pearl City** (641 Jackson St., tel. 415/398–8383) is a good choice, as is the low-key, hidden-feeling **Hang Ah** (1 Pagoda Pl., at Sacramento St., tel 415/982–5686). **Great Eastern** (649 Jackson St., tel. 415/986–2500) has excellent fresh seafood, exemplified by their fish tanks.

COIT TOWER AND TELEGRAPH HILL

Folklore has it that 210-foot Coit Tower, which crowns the crest of 248-foot Telegraph Hill, was built to resemble the end of a fire hose. This may be a myth, but there's some logic to it: The stone-white concrete tower was intended as a monument to the city's volunteer firefighters. (Lillie Hitchcock Coit, who bequeathed the funds that paid for it, was a wealthy and eccentric heiress with a passion for fire engines—and firemen.) Since 1933, when it was completed, the tower has become one of San Francisco's most distinctive landmarks, with only the Golden Gate Bridge and perhaps the Transamerica Pyramid more recognized as symbols of the city.

Coit Tower also offers some of San Francisco's best views—an exciting panorama of hills, islands, bridges, and the bay spreading out below. The 360-degree vista from the top of the tower's Observation Gallery, reached by elevator, is the most encompassing; however, if you come in the evening after the Observation Gallery has closed—when the tower is lighted up like a beacon—or you don't want to ride to the top, you can simply enjoy the

MAKE THE MOST OF YOUR TIME The view is the number-one reason to visit Coit Tower, so set off on a clear day. If you're driving and you can manage to avoid the weekend, you shouldn't have much trouble parking (though sunny summer days are another matter). Even kids interested in the WPA-era murals in the tower will likely need no more than an hour here. The grassy park behind the tower is good for letting off steam, and there's plenty of shopping and dining in North Beach to round out a visit. For grown-ups perhaps the best part of a visit to the tower is the lovely descent down the Filbert Steps, bordered by lush private gardens and sweet turn-of-the-century bungalows.

Telegraph Hill Blvd. at
Greenwich or Lombard Sts.

 Elevator $4.50 ages 13
and up, $2 children 6–12

 Observation Gallery daily 10–6

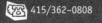 415/362-0808

 6 and up

free views outside. Inside the tower, on the ground floor, are murals that were painted by 25 artists as a public works project during the Depression; they depict California's working people in a socialist-realist style pioneered by Mexican artist Diego Rivera.

If your kids are good walkers—don't try this with a stroller—you can opt for either of two easy-to-overlook routes to go back down the hill. Both the Filbert Steps and Greenwich Steps, steep staircase walks that parallel each other as they lead down toward the bay from the east side of Telegraph Hill, are flanked by terraced gardens and secluded homes. While you're taking in more great views of the bay on the way down, your kids can play explorer—as long as they stay out of the residents' gardens.

If you like this sight you may also like Golden Gate Park (#41).

KEEP IN MIND

While you're wandering the grounds around Coit Tower, keep your eyes—and ears—peeled for the flock of wild parrots that roosts here. The bright green, red-headed birds make quite a racket. No handouts, though: To protect the wild birds, the city council banned feeding them in 2007.

EATS FOR KIDS Pick up picnic supplies at **Molinari's** (373 Columbus Ave., tel. 415/421–2337), a colorful Italian deli in North Beach, and then have a feast in Washington Square Park. **Tommaso's** (1042 Kearny St., tel. 415/398–9696) crisp, thin-crust pizzas may be San Francisco's all-time favorite. You may have to wait for a table, so come early (dinner only; no reservations). **Mo's Gourmet Hamburgers** (1322 Grant Ave., tel. 415/788–3779), in North Beach, serves up, you guessed it, a variety of big, juicy burgers in casual surroundings.

COYOTE POINT PARK AND MUSEUM

A wooded lick jutting into the bay about 2 miles south of San Francisco International Airport, Coyote Point Park can easily be an all-day destination. You'll find tree-shaded walking trails with bay overlooks, bike paths, picnic areas, playfields and playgrounds, a fishing jetty, a marina, a summer swimming beach, a saltwater marsh, an adjacent public golf course, and a highly regarded nature museum.

Even on a nice day, be sure to leave some time for the Coyote Point Museum for Environmental Education. Here, your kids can see live animals native to the Bay Area displayed in realistic habitats, mostly behind glass—think reptile house at the zoo. Look for a river otter, burrowing owl, porcupine, badger, raccoons, skunks, birds of prey, toads, snakes, lizards, a bobcat— even lowly banana slugs. A walk-through outdoor aviary provides close-up looks at a variety of birds.

KEEP IN MIND For some kids, the proximity of the airport is the most exciting thing about Coyote Point. The overlook outside the museum gives front-row seats to planes taking off and landing, endlessly fascinating for children of a certain age.

MAKE THE MOST OF YOUR TIME On a sunny weekend day it's wise to arrive early to beat the crowds. About the only thing lacking at Coyote Point, besides roller coasters and pizza stands, is enough parking to accommodate all the family cars pouring in for a day's fun in the sunshine. Small children—and older kids not particularly interested in ecology—may make quick work of the museum. If you can, time your visit to take in the daily otter feeding (usually at 12:30) or frequent fox talks (usually at 11:30). Though the museum itself is mostly indoors, much of the fun stuff is outdoors; save this one for a long, sunny day.

Park, bay side of U.S. 101, San Mateo; museum, 1651 Coyote Point Dr., San Mateo

 Park $5 per car. Museum $6 adults, $4 youths 13–17, $2 children 3–12; 1st W of mth free

 Park daily sunrise–sunset; museum T–Sa 10–5, Su 12–5

650/573–2592 park, 650/342–7755 museum; www.coyoteptmuseum.org

3 and up

Along with lots of light and space and fun-to-follow wooden ramps connecting the displays, the museum contains low-key interactive exhibits and an Environmental Hall that leads you through the Bay Area's major ecosystems: redwood forest, chaparral, grassland, oak woodland, baylands, and coastal. It's like taking a walk from the Santa Cruz Mountains to the Pacific Ocean (but a lot easier on your feet). Though the museum is especially well suited to school-age kids, any child 3 or older can enjoy at least the animal displays.

Pick up a flyer on current museum events for families, which might include periodic Family Activity Days and wildlife shows. Also check for temporary exhibitions, which often include wild animals and hands-on displays and may warrant a visit all by themselves. In summer, five-day Summer Discovery Camps let kids 7–10 meet animals, go tide-pooling at an ocean beach, and go hiking, too.

If you like this site you may also like the Lindsay Wildlife Museum (#33).

EATS FOR KIDS The park contains several picnic areas near the water; if you have a large group, you can call to reserve tables. The museum itself has a pleasant outdoor picnic area surrounded by gardens. In nearby Burlingame, the **Copenhagen Bakery** (1216 Burlingame Ave., tel. 650/342–1357) has sandwiches you can take out. Also in Burlingame, friendly and casual **Pizza Italia Café** (321 Primrose Rd., tel. 650/343–4444) makes great focaccia sandwiches, pasta, and pizza, all available to go.

THE EMBARCADERO

If San Francisco's 1989 earthquake had one positive effect, it was the subsequent tearing down of the quake-damaged Embarcadero Freeway. For decades, that elevated river of concrete had obscured bay views and blocked the sunlight along this 3-mile, bayside route. Now the area has blossomed into a promenade for walkers, runners, rollerbladers, renegade skateboarders, sun worshippers, restaurant goers, and those who simply wish to gaze out at the endless procession of sailboats, tugboats, barges, freighters, ferries, cruise ships—and the occasional submarine—on their way from port to port or out to sea.

The centerpiece of the Embarcadero, at the foot of Market Street, is the historic, century-old Ferry Building. Its 230-foot clock tower, once the tallest structure west of the Mississippi, remains a distinctive city landmark. Though it's still a departure point for ferries to the East and North bays, today its street-level gourmet marketplace is one of the city's favorite places to dine and shop for organic produce, artisan cheeses, and local meat and seafood. Its rear boardwalk is a prime bay-gazing spot. Across from the Ferry Building, Justin Herman

MAKE THE MOST OF YOUR TIME The Embarcadero actually
stretches all the way from Fisherman's Wharf to the ballpark, far too long a walk for most kids.
With older kids, the Embarcadero makes a terrific bike ride. Start the morning at the wharf,
taking in the ships at the Hyde Street Pier, the Musée Mecanique, and whatever else strikes
your fancy. Then head south, stopping at the Ferry Building for lunch and perhaps a look at
the San Francisco Railway Museum. Continue south along the water to China Basin, the ballpark, and more great views. If you don't want to cycle or your kids are younger, take the
F-line from the Wharf to the Ferry Building, then continue on the T-Third to the ballpark.

Plaza is the site of the 30-foot-wide Vallaincourt Fountain and, in winter, an outdoor ice rink. At the F-line stop on the plaza, the free San Francisco Railway Museum gives kids a close-up view of the city's vintage trolleys. Next to the plaza begin the five skyscrapers of the Embarcadero Center (tel. 800/733–6318), which house shops and restaurants.

The Embarcadero is lined with piers, most now put to purposes other than shipping. South of the Ferry Building, all piers are even numbered; to the north, they're odd numbered. Just north of the Ferry Building, a boardwalk follows newly restored Piers 1, 3 ½, and 5, while Pier 7 is a public promenade lined with vintage lampposts and benches. Its wooden-plank pier, the city's longest, is ideal for fishing, eating a picnic lunch, and offers some of the best photo-ops in town.

If you like this sight you may also like Fisherman's Wharf (#45).

KEEP IN MIND

If there's a baseball game going on but you don't want to buy tickets, you can catch a few innings for free in the standing-room area between the ballpark and the water. Even if you're not among them, it's fun to watch the very adventurous folks in boats waiting to catch "splash hits," home runs that fly over the wall into the bay.

EATS FOR KIDS The Ferry Building is a veritable gourmet wonderland, great for gathering (expensive) picnic supplies, but the sit-down places here are best for older kids. Just north, kid-friendly **Pancho Villa Taqueria** (Pier 1, tel. 415/982–2182) serves huge portions of reliable Mexican food, also to go. A block from the ballpark, look for Caribbean-color **Primo Patio Café** (214 Townsend St., 415/957–1129), where yummy, reasonably priced Caribbean-inspired food—and great drinks for the grown-ups—on the sunny patio feels like a day in the islands.

EXPLORATORIUM

Most kids' eyes light up as soon as they enter the Exploratorium. Set in the Marina District, it's one of the world's top science museums, drawing more than 500,000 visitors per year, and an absolute can't-miss with young people. More than 650 hands-on exhibits invite curious kids and parents to test and investigate mysteries of science and human perception—how we see, hear, smell, and feel the world around us. Light, color, sound, music, motion, language, electricity, and weather are among the subject areas.

What's that cloud ring rising into the air? A 5-year-old boy made it in the Weather area. How did that 7-year-old girl leave her shadow on the wall? Your kids can capture their own shadows in the Shadow Box. Look at that 10-year-old. He's as tall as the ceiling, but only in the Distorted Room. How did that family make the Enchanted Tree light up? Just by clapping their hands. Kids can try finger painting via computer, touch a miniature tornado, and blow giant soap bubbles, too. "Explainers"—often high-school students on their days off—offer help and demonstrations ("Cow-eye dissection starting over here!").

KEEP IN MIND Across Lyon Street in the Presidio, George Lucas's Letterman Digital Arts Center has beautifully landscaped public grounds. Star Wars fans will want to visit the Yoda Fountain and peek into the building behind it to see a life-size Darth Vader.

MAKE THE MOST OF YOUR TIME The Exploratorium is the perfect rainy-day place, but on sunny days there's tons to do outside. The Exploratorium is on the grounds of the Palace of Fine Arts, a neoclassical domed and pillared beauty. The palace rises alongside a lovely tree-shaded lagoon occupied by mallards and swans, with benches and sloping grassy hillsides. Across Marina Boulevard and to the east is the yacht-lined Marina Green (#30), and the harbor's Wave Organ, an Exploratorium project.

3601 Lyon St., near Baker St. and Marina Blvd. (parking at Lyon and Bay Sts.)

 $14 adults, $11 college students and youths 13–17, $9 children 4–12; 1st W of mth free

 T–Su 10–5

415/397–5673, 415/561–0362 Tactile Dome; www.exploratorium.edu

 2 and up

In Playlab, infants and toddlers can play with blocks and develop motor skills on a climbing structure. The Exploratorium also features two or three intriguing temporary exhibits each year, exploring topics as varied as memory and flea circuses.

A separate area, the Tactile Dome, requires reservations (one to six weeks in advance), an additional fee, and a sense of adventure. In this pitch-black maze set inside a geodesic dome, the challenge—and the fun—is to crawl, slide, and climb through it relying entirely on your sense of touch. Kids should be at least 8 and not afraid of the dark; it's also not recommended for pregnant women or anyone who's claustrophobic. It takes about 15 minutes to work your way through once, but many inquisitive young explorers go through two or three times. By then your child will be ready to come back into the light and experience all five senses at this extraordinary museum.

If you like this site you may also like the California Academy of Sciences (#57).

EATS FOR KIDS The **Exploratorium Café** (tel. 415/921–8603) has such lunch items as organic salads and tuna or smoked turkey sandwiches for lunch. Grab a fresh, seriously stacked sandwich at the counter of **Lucca Delicatessen** (2120 Chestnut St., tel. 415/921–7873) and you're set for a picnic by the pond before you head inside the museum. Great veggie and meaty curries are served up at **Taste of the Himalayas** (2420 Lombard St., tel. 415/674–9898), a casual space with mask-adorned walls.

FARALLON ISLAND NATURE CRUISE

On a clear day, from points along the western edges of San Francisco, you can usually see the Farallon Islands jutting up from the Pacific, 27 miles off the Golden Gate. Even most longtime San Franciscans, however, have never seen the Farallones close up—or have a clue as to the extraordinary display of wildlife that's out there. The seven islands, comprising the Farallon National Wildlife Refuge, are home to 23 species of marine mammals, including thousands of harbor seals, California sea lions, Steller's sea lions, and Northern elephant seals. And up to 300,000 breeding seabirds visit the islands annually, making this the largest Pacific seabird rookery south of Alaska.

Only small groups of researchers are allowed on the refuge at a time. The public isn't allowed to set foot in this fragile environment, sometimes called "the most exclusive neighborhood in San Francisco" (the islands are within city and county limits). But you can get excellent views of the islands' rocky slopes from the deck of an Oceanic Society Expeditions boat.

MAKE THE MOST OF YOUR TIME

This is a trip you definitely need to prepare for ahead of time. Ensure that your family has warm and waterproof clothing, since trips depart rain or shine. Be certain of your children's seaworthiness before embarking, as there's no turning back. Kids should have sailed on the ocean at least once before going. Take seasickness precautions, and bring binoculars, sunglasses, and sunscreen, even if the weather is foggy at departure. (You're less likely to encounter foggy weather in fall than in summer.)

Oceanic Society Expeditions,
Ft. Mason Center, Bldg. E

 $95

Departures May–Nov, S–Su 8 AM

415/474–3385 or 800/326–7491;
www.oceanic-society.org

10 and up

The eight-hour Farallon Island Nature Cruise (reservations required), aboard one of three Coast Guard–certified vessels, departs from San Francisco's San Francisco Yacht Harbor, at the Marina Green (#30). The trip is for adults and children 10 and over only, since the seas can get rough and the winds very cold. Expert naturalists point out wildlife and answer questions. Chances are a number of Dall porpoises will escort the boat, darting around, past, and under the bow in a sort of exhilarating joyride. Whales are a common sight: humpbacks with flukes shooting high in the air as they dive, and even blue whales, the largest mammals ever on earth. The granite islands themselves are alive with birds, their shrieking and squawking surrounding you in natural stereo, while a parcel of barking sea lions typically provides the basso profundo.

If you like this experience you may also like Bay Cruises (#60).

KEEP IN MIND

In fall the Farallones are a favorite feeding ground of white sharks, attracted by the abundance of marine mammals who gather here. For the super adventurous (and wealthy), **Great White Adventures** (tel. 510/814–8256) leads 12-hour tours out of Emeryville in the East Bay. You can get up close and personal in a cage dive ($775) or watch topside ($375).

EATS FOR KIDS You'll need to bring snacks, lunch, and drinks for the boat trip since there's no galley on board. For dinner, **Greens** (Ft. Mason Center, Bldg. A, tel. 415/771–6222) is an excellent vegetarian restaurant, good for older kids. It has terrific bay views, but you'll need reservations, or grab takeout from **Greens to Go** (tel. 415/771–6330). **Mels Drive-In** (2165 Lombard St., tel. 415/921–2867) serves up burgers, curly fries, milk shakes, and cherry Cokes with '50s decor and jukeboxes. Kids' meals come in toy Corvettes. **Lucca Delicatessen** (2120 Chestnut St., tel. 415/921–7873) builds fantastic sandwiches to go.

FISHERMAN'S WHARF

Fisherman's Wharf is no longer the thriving fishing center it was a century ago. Modern-day catches have been ravaged by overfishing and pollution. Today the historic waterfront district, a now loosely defined area that runs for eight or nine blocks from Aquatic Park to Pier 39 (#19), relies mainly on tourism for revenues. It's the city's number-one tourist attraction, crowds can be overwhelming (come in the morning if possible), and the last remnants of the real working wharf can be hard to find amid the hodgepodge of attractions—some maritime-related, some not, and many overpriced. These include schlocky souvenir stands, novelty museums, and often-mediocre seafood restaurants. For all these reasons, many locals avoid it. Still, it's a noisy, active place that kids tend to like.

KEEP IN MIND Keep your eyes peeled for the Bushman, a local legend who hides behind a palm frond on the sidewalk and shouts "Ugga bugga!" at unwary passersby to the delight—and donations—of bystanders.

To glimpse real fishermen at work, head for Richard Henry Dana Street (better known as "Fish Alley"), but remember that fishermen work early. Some other authentic sights at the Wharf are provided on a bevy of historic ships berthed there. The Hyde Street Pier (#39) includes a fascinating collection of boats, and you can tour two World

MAKE THE MOST OF YOUR TIME Entertaining for most adults, though kids like it, too, is the wonderful Musée Mecanique (Pier 45), with vintage games and novelties. One of the most pleasant times to visit the wharf is in the evening during the Christmas holidays, when many fishing boats twinkle with lights; look across the bay from here to see the lighted cross atop the peak of Angel Island. Also, although there are public parking lots near the Wharf, you'll pay dearly for most of them (check for validation options). It's cheaper (and more fun) to take a cable car or trolley.

Bounded by Aquatic Park, North Point, Powell St., and Pier 39

415/626–7070;
www.fishermanswharf.org

Free; some attractions charge

Daily 24 hrs; attractions shorter hrs

5 and up

War II vessels berthed at Pier 45. Along the boardwalk, historic markers tell the history of the wharf.

Free entertainment is often here, too, in the form of street performers—jugglers, musicians, magicians—one of the best bargains around even if you drop some coins in their hats. You can usually find them on sidewalks or at the area's four main shopping centers: the Cannery, Ghirardelli Square, Pier 39, and the Anchorage. The Cannery began as the world's largest peach-canning plant in 1907 and today is a rather desolate mall (home to the Basic Brown Bear Factory—#62). Ghirardelli Square was once a chocolate factory, bustling today with specialty shops, restaurants, and cheesy galleries. Like everywhere else at the Wharf, you'll have plenty of company here from other families, who come from around the world to soak up the atmosphere—and try to avoid bumping into each other.

If you like this site you may also like the Embarcadero (#48).

EATS FOR KIDS It's hard to resist the stands with bubbling **crab pots** on Jefferson Street for a crab or shrimp cocktail, even if many are skimpy for the price. Two good fish restaurants are **A. Sabella's** (2766 Taylor St., tel. 415/771–6775), which serves seafood and pasta with an extensive children's menu, and **Alioto's** (8 Fisherman's Wharf, tel. 415/673–0183), with old-time atmosphere and seafood that really does match the views.

FT. FUNSTON

Where's the fort at Ft. Funston? You won't find a walled fortress or cannons here. The military did, however, once stake a claim to this area of windswept sands just south of Ocean Beach (#21), along the western reaches of San Francisco.

Since the early 1900s, and through two world wars, the Army used the high cliffs at Ft. Funston as a strategic lookout and a base for heavy weaponry protecting San Francisco Bay from attack. During World War II, Ft. Funston's Battery Davis sported guns weighing almost 150 tons each; there's one 146-tonner you can still see today. During the Cold War, the current parking lot was the site of a Nike missile battery. But since the Army pulled out some years ago, all that remains of its legacy are gun emplacements gathering rust in the foggy mists.

Today Ft. Funston is part of the Golden Gate National Recreation Area, and where guns once pointed out to the Pacific, rangers and volunteers now run a nursery for native plants and lead environmental education programs for schoolkids. What's more, the last of the

MAKE THE MOST OF YOUR TIME The best months for watching hang gliders are late March through October; avoid a rainy day, though this part of town is often socked in with fog. Though rare, crashes have occurred at the hang-gliding observation deck, so it's a good idea to keep an eye out—and up. Some other safety suggestions: In general, keep your kids away from cliff edges, dress warmly, and beware of riptides at the beach, if you manage to make the steep hike down.

undeveloped dunes that once blanketed much of the coast are still preserved here. You and your children can hike to the beach below or watch from a viewing deck as hang gliders take off from the cliffs and soar through the skies. The Sunset Trail, a 1-mile paved loop that links up to the Coastal Trail going north along Ocean Beach, traverses the cliffs and provides sea views. As its name suggests, this is one of the best places in San Francisco to watch the sun go down—at least when it's not clouded with coastal fog. Stay on marked trails: Some of the roads you may see here actually go nowhere. They were built to confuse the enemy in wartime, but thankfully, no enemies ever invaded. And Ft. Funston remains enough off the beaten track that crowds never invade here, either. It makes for a nice spot to wander among dunes and enjoy nature without leaving the city.

If you like this site you may also like China Beach (#52) and Ft. Point National Historic Site (#43).

EATS FOR KIDS There are picnic tables but no food concessions here, and though there are no eating places in the immediate vicinity of Ft. Funston, you can find some a few minutes' drive away. Among the closest are those across from the San Francisco Zoo on Sloat Boulevard. Family-run **Pasquale's Pizza** (2640 Sloat Blvd., tel. 415/566-7772) serves up tasty pizza, especially the thin crust, also to go.

KEEP IN MIND
As you walk along the dunes between March and August, keep an eye out for bank swallows' nests high in the sheer faces. Entire colonies dig holes right into the cliffs to lay eggs and raise their young, who fly off in late summer.

FT. POINT NATIONAL HISTORIC SITE

43

Dramatically situated beneath the southern stretches of the Golden Gate Bridge on San Francisco Bay, Ft. Point is the only brick fort you can visit in the western United States. Built during the Civil War to help protect San Francisco from sea attack—it was modeled after Ft. Sumter in South Carolina and completed in 1861—the massive fort could hold as many as 500 soldiers and 126 cannons. During World War II, soldiers stood watch here as part of the coastal defense of California. Today it's part of Presidio National Park (#17) and a good place to immerse kids in some local military history while soaking up breathtaking vistas of the bay below and the bridge overhead.

The best views are from the roof of the fort, where your kids can pretend they're searching for enemy ships. More likely, they'll spot windsurfers braving the waves here or freighters passing through the Golden Gate. Just to the east, where the surf crashes into the rocks below the walkway, is the spot where Jimmy Stewart pulled Kim Novak out of the water in the Hitchcock film *Vertigo* (a good video to watch with older kids before visiting).

KEEP IN MIND If your kids are seriously into battlements ask the ranger at the fort or the folks at the visitor center to point you toward other military remnants in the Presidio. Then you may want to head over to the cemetery to walk among the soldiers' graves; the earliest dates to 1849, when the Presidio was already a military installation.

MAKE THE MOST OF YOUR TIME Visitors rave about candlelight tours of the fort, offered by reservation Saturday evenings November through February; it's a trip back in time, recommended for kids 10 and over. Visiting the fort anytime can be vertigo-inducing, and the higher points can feel downright dangerous on windy days. To watch the kids run without holding your breath, head down just east of Ft. Point to the Presidio's Crissy Field. After two years of restoring native plants and dunes, the National Park Service reopened this shoreline park in 2001, with a bookstore–café, two nature centers, beach access, and trails for walkers, cyclists, runners, and skaters.

Even though Ft. Point was well equipped with cannons, none have ever been fired in anger here. But national park rangers conduct cannon-loading demonstrations on an 1862-era field artillery piece every day, and it's a complex, fascinating process. (Call the fort for the daily schedule.) Your family can also visit the rooms that lie off the restored central courtyard to see museum-style exhibits of American military memorabilia and watch a film containing old newsreel footage of the building of the Golden Gate Bridge. Twice a year docents dressed in Civil War–era costumes give tours and costumed Civil War enthusiasts mill about, adding to the historical flavor.

If you like this sight you may also like Alcatraz Island (#67) and Ft. Funston (#44).

EATS FOR KIDS Crissy Field and other areas of the Presidio make nice picnic spots. Within Crissy Field, the **Warming Hut** (W. Crissy Field Dr., tel. 415/561–3042) serves fresh sandwiches and has plenty of relatively healthy kid snacks; their hot chocolate is perfect for a chilly day.

GOLDEN GATE BRIDGE

It's the symbol of San Francisco and probably the most celebrated and photographed bridge in the world. Completed in 1937 after four years of construction, the Golden Gate Bridge is still one of the world's longest suspension bridges, stretching across the straits (aka the Golden Gate) from San Francisco north to Marin County. Its two towers rise 750 feet into the air, and it uses enough cable wire to wrap around the equator three times. More than 40 million vehicles cross it each year. You can drive across the bridge, too, of course, but the best way to see it—and the views from it—is to walk across.

Pedestrians can ride the No. 28 Muni bus to the bridge and get off at the toll plaza. If you drive, park your car either at the lot on the San Francisco side or at Vista Point, on the Marin side, and set out on foot along the walkway that runs along the eastern (bay side) of the bridge. Bring plenty of quarters for the parking meters and make sure everyone dresses warmly, even on sunny days, because the winds can whip fiercely across the bridge and you never know when the damp fog will come swirling in. Though the bridge is 1.7 miles

MAKE THE MOST OF YOUR TIME If your kids are old enough and good cyclists, you can ride bikes across the bridge. Bikers are limited to the west (ocean) side of the bridge on weekends and weekday afternoons and evenings. Experienced cyclists might consider continuing to Sausalito, in Marin County, for more bay-side views or to explore the town. Just follow the bike lane at the end of the Vista Point parking lot to Alexander Avenue, but realize that once off the bridge, you'll be sharing the road with cars. Lots of folks bike over the bridge and take a ferry back from Sausalito. If you're walking, you might consider combining a walk on the bridge with a visit to Ft. Point (#43), just below.

Hwy. 1 and U.S. 101 north (from Marina, take Doyle Dr. from Marina Blvd.)

 Pedestrians, bikes, and northbound cars free; southbound cars $5

 Daily 24 hrs bikes and cars, 5 AM–9 PM pedestrians

415/921–5858; www.goldengatebridge.org

4 and up

long (including approaches), you don't need to cover the full distance to get the full effect. It's a thrill just to get a few hundred feet out onto the bridge, which stands 220 feet above the water. You'll feel the rush of air as cars whiz by and feel the bridge sway in the wind. In fact, it can sway as much as 27½ feet east to west.

Linger as long as you want—and as your kids will allow—to see the views of the city skyline, Alcatraz, Angel Island, Ft. Point, the Marin Headlands, and a passing parade of sailboats, freighters, and windsurfers. Times when fog is swirling about are especially magical, but whenever you go, it's an unforgettable experience.

If you like this site you may also like Coit Tower (#50) and the Embarcadero (#48).

KEEP IN MIND

Railings on the bridge are currently only 4 feet tall, though there's much discussion about adding a suicide barrier to stop people from jumping (which happens about once every two weeks). It can be unnerving to see little ones poking their heads over the tops and walking close to bridge traffic whizzing by the flimsy barrier, so stay close together and keep an eye out for cyclists.

EATS FOR KIDS The closest San Francisco restaurants are in the Richmond and Marina districts. **Giorgio's Pizzeria** (151 Clement St., tel. 415/668–1266), in the Richmond, is a longtime contender for the city's best pizza.

GOLDEN GATE PARK

You could probably spend every weekend for a year in 3-mile-long, ½-mile-wide Golden Gate Park and still miss at least one corner of it. Though fraying a bit around the edges—cutbacks in public funds mean fewer gardeners and maintenance people and more homeless "campers"—this remains one of America's most beautiful urban parks, filled with lakes, flowers, and meadows.

Most attractions are clustered in the eastern half of the park, including the outstanding California Academy of Sciences (#57) and, across the way, the de Young Museum. In front of the museum is the Music Concourse, where the park band plays free concerts on Sunday afternoons. Just down the road is the Japanese Tea Garden, with arched bridges, koi fish ponds, and a towering red pagoda. Across from the Tea Garden, San Francisco Botanical Garden displays flowers, redwoods, cacti, and other flora from around the world; don't miss the duck pond near the entrance.

KEEP IN MIND The park's gorgeous **Conservatory of Flowers** ($5 adults, $3 ages 12–17, $1.50 ages 5–11) captures kids' imaginations with its aquatic plants room, replete with gigantic lily pads and carnivorous plants.

MAKE THE MOST OF YOUR TIME One great half day is taking in the view from the de Young's observation tower (free), exploring the Japanese Tea Garden ($4 ages 6 and over, $1.50 ages 5 and under), and picnicking at the San Francisco Botanical Garden (free). If you like to bike or go rollerblading with your kids, the best time to visit Golden Gate Park is on Sunday, when Kennedy Drive is closed to cars between Stanyan Street and 19th Avenue and cyclists and rollerbladers take over. In all, the park has more than 7 miles of paved roads and trails to follow. A number of places nearby rent bikes and skates.

Bounded by Fulton and Stanyan Sts., Lincoln Way, and Great Hwy.

 Free; some attractions charge

 Daily 6 AM–10 PM

415/831-2700, 415/752-4227 Japanese Tea Garden; www.nps.gov/goga

 All ages

Just up Martin Luther King Jr. Drive is pretty Stow Lake, where you can picnic and rent rowboats and pedalboats. With older kids, cross footbridges to hilly Strawberry Island, in the middle of the lake, and hike to the top to peer over the crest of Huntington Falls, which plunges 125 feet—the West's highest artificial waterfall. Nearby, the Rhododendron Dell blazes with color in spring. In the park's southeast corner, younger kids flock to the newly renovated Koret Children's Quarter (off Kezar or Bowling Green drives) to explore tide pools, climb wave walls, and scale plain old play structures; the adjacent 1912 Herschel-Spillman Carousel spins with 62 hand-carved animals. The park's western half is more woodsy and pastoral, best explored by bike. Toward the ocean (along Kennedy Drive), you can visit a herd of bison at the Bison Paddock and hike, bike, or stroll along quiet tree-lined trails.

If you like this site you may also like the Presidio (#17) and Tilden Park (#6).

EATS FOR KIDS Picnic spots abound in the park. Some of the best include Stow Lake, the San Francisco Botanical Garden, and the various meadows along John F. Kennedy Drive west of 19th Avenue. Staff in traditional costume serve tea and cookies at the **Teahouse** (Japanese Tea Garden, Tea Garden Dr., tel. 415/752-1171). Open to the public, the **de Young Café** (50 Hagiwara Tea Garden Dr., tel. 415/750-2614) serves good snacks and entrées made with locally grown ingredients; choose a table inside or outdoors in the sculpture garden.

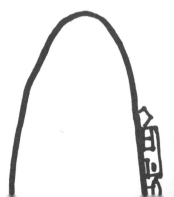

HILLER AVIATION MUSEUM

If the aviation buffs in your family long to climb into the cockpit of a jumbo jet or a Blue Angel, they'll be flying high at the Hiller Aviation Museum, backing the tarmac of the San Carlos airport. With lots of hands-on exhibits, video accompanying most aircraft, and posed mannequins dressed according to the styles of the times the aircraft were built— a lively touch—this compact museum of flight appeals to kids young and old.

You'll first stop for tickets, which, for better or worse, are sold in the large gift shop. The exhibits themselves kick off with the Aviator, the first controlled powered flight vehicle; built in 1869, it predates the Wright Brothers and looks like a hot-air balloon that's been pinched underneath. Other fun aircraft include early helicopters like the Rotocycle, with very little around the pilot; a beautifully restored 1935 Fairchild 22 prop plane, all set to sweep a couple off on their honeymoon; and experimental aircraft straight out of science fiction, like Nasa's Swing Wing, which looks like it was put together incorrectly.

MAKE THE MOST OF YOUR TIME The museum is rarely crowded, though weekdays offer the best opportunity for spending time on the simulators. And except for standing on the outdoor platform overlooking the runways, this is a good bet for a rainy day. Check the museum's Web site for discount coupons.

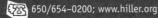

Despite the impressive presentation and fancy aircraft, most kids run straight from one hands-on exhibit to another. You can climb into (half of) a Boeing supersonic airplane, a UH-12 helicopter, and a Blue Angel cockpit; try your luck with a flying-platform simulator (as odd as it sounds) or a climb-in flight simulator that rocks and pitches—especially when you crash. Head upstairs to an observation area overlooking the runways of the San Carlos Airport and tune in to control-tower communications. Another blockbuster exhibit awaits out back: the forward section of a restored 747, including first class upstairs, business class, and the cockpit, complete with a pilot to answer your questions.

If you like this sight you may also like the U.S.S. *Hornet* (#5).

KEEP IN MIND

Get ready to do some advanced gift buying at the Hiller Aviation Museum's well-stocked shop. From small flight-related toys, books, and sticker treats for the youngest kids—great for distraction on trips—to huge Lego and Play-mobil sets and a robust selection of models for grade-school ages, it's the largest collection of all things flight-related in the Bay Area.

EATS FOR KIDS Continue the aviation theme at **Sky Kitchen** (620 Airport Dr., tel. 650/595-0464), the diner at the San Carlos Airport. Watch planes take off and land at the airport outside and choose from a long list of solid breakfast items and standard lunch fare in the company of pilots telling tales of flight.

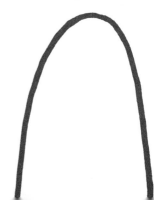

HYDE STREET PIER

39

Rising high above the water at Aquatic Park, the towering masts of the historic ships berthed here bring you back to a time when swashbuckling buccaneers, fierce pirates, and jaundiced sailors patrolled the seas. This pier, part of the San Francisco Maritime National Historic Park and the country's only floating national park, is a great spot to introduce kids to what shipboard life was like in the days before *The Queen Mary 2* or even the *Titanic*.

Of the five historic vessels docked here, three can be boarded. Kids gravitate toward the three tall masts of the *Balclutha,* an 1886 steel-hulled, square-rigged sailing ship. The 300-foot-long windjammer was launched in Scotland and navigated Cape Horn 17 times before ending its days transporting Alaskan salmon from the Bering Sea to San Francisco (when it was known as the *Star of Alaska*). When the ship isn't being restored, kids can get a taste of sailor life by clambering down its narrow ladders and around its claustrophobic decks and peeking at its restored cabins (the captain's quarters are particularly impressive). Follow a ranger below deck on San Francisco Bay's oldest ferry, the

KEEP IN MIND Historic vessels need lots of restoration, work that can go on for years, and if your family is anxious to see a particular ship, call ahead to check her status; for instance, the *Balclutha*—always a highlight—is now closed, with no projected finish date. Despite the closures, the pier merits a visit.

MAKE THE MOST OF YOUR TIME Kids dig the real ship-wrecked boat and gigantic First Order Fresnel lighthouse lens on display at the San Francisco Maritime National Historic Park's Visitor Center (499 Jefferson St., tel. 415/447–5000), a quick, fun add-on to a visit to the historic ships across the street. The sandy beach at Aquatic Park (tel. 415/556–1238), just below the National Maritime Museum, is a good place to run around or relax after touring the ships or museum. Kids can wade in the gentle (though cold) water and wonder at the hardy souls of the park's resident Dolphin Club. The Municipal Pier, a favored fishing spot, is nearby.

paddle wheeler *Eureka*; it dates from 1890 and was once the world's largest auto and passenger ferry. For some kids, the vintage car collection onboard is the highlight of a visit here. The *Hercules,* a steam-powered ocean tug that is boardable at high tide only. Take a quick peek at the exteriors of the 1891 scow schooner *Alma,* with a flat bottom that enabled her to navigate the shallow waters on the periphery of the bay, where she hauled hay, and the *C.A. Thayer,* a three-masted schooner built in 1895 to move the lumber that helped build many early California cities. Special events—sail-raisings, sea chantey songfests, evening concerts—are held here periodically, and frequently on summer weekends. Housed in a 1930s art deco building and part of the national historic park, the worthwhile National Maritime Museum is closed for renovation and scheduled to reopen in 2009.

If you like this site you may also like Fisherman's Wharf (#45).

EATS FOR KIDS You can spread out a blanket and picnic at Aquatic Park, where you can also find **snack bars.** Just above the park, at the popular Ghirardelli Square shopping complex (N. Point St.), the **Ghirardelli Chocolate Manufactory and Soda Fountain** (tel. 415/474–3938) draws hordes of families who come to gorge on huge sundaes, floats, and other chocolate concoctions. (Lines can be brutally long at peak tourist hours.) You can still watch chocolate being made in original vats and ovens in the old-fashioned ice-cream parlor.

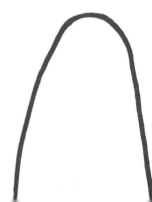

JAPANTOWN

Japantown is the focal point for San Francisco's residents of Japanese descent, who first settled this area after the 1906 earthquake. As the Japanese built churches, shrines, shops, and restaurants, the neighborhood began to take on the look of a miniature Ginza and became known as Nihonmachi or Japantown. Its commercial heart is the Japan Center (Post and Buchanan Sts.)—a three-square-block complex of shops, restaurants, teahouses, hotels, pastry shops, movie theaters, Japanese baths, and more, all connected by walkways. The five-tiered, 100-foot-high pagoda crowning its Peace Plaza and a few fountains lend the center some Japanese flair, but overall it's spare and uninspiring. Bring the kids here to check out those quirky details that make foreign travel exciting: eyeing the plastic food displays in restaurant windows, shopping for CDs, leafing through Japanese graphic novels, and examining exotic vending machines offerings—puffy stickers with photos of you on them, anyone? They can also look for flying-fish kites, miniature notepads, and other colorful items from Japan in the shops.

MAKE THE MOST OF YOUR TIME Other than the Cherry Blossom Festival, the best time to visit Japantown is on a weekend afternoon—around lunchtime, of course—when the shops and restaurants are all open and the area is lively (it can feel a bit deserted). Street parking can be difficult, but the Japan Center has two big indoor parking garages. Most stores, restaurants, and theaters will validate parking. Alternately, take Muni's No. 38 Geary bus, which runs between Union Square and the Richmond District and stops at Japantown.

Bounded by Geary Blvd. and
Fillmore, Laguna, and Bush Sts.

415/922-6776 Japan Center,
415/563-2313 Cherry Blossom Festival;
www.sfjapantown.org

Free

Most shops daily 10–6,
Japan Center daily 10–10

6 and up

A 135-foot covered bridge lined with shops and a restaurant—kids get a kick of eating over the street—crosses over Webster Street between two of the commercial buildings. It's a wonderful spot to browse, as is the Buchanan Mall, which runs for a block along Buchanan Street between Sutter and Post streets. More attractive than the Japan Center, it's a pedestrian-only mall with cobbled streets, flowering plum and cherry trees, and several restaurants.

The highlight of the year in Japantown is the Nihonmachi Cherry Blossom Festival, held during two weekends each April. A dazzling, 2½-hour parade—running 15 blocks from City Hall to the Japan Center—caps the second weekend.

If you like this sight you may also like Chinatown (#51) as well as the Mission and North Beach neighborhoods.

EATS FOR KIDS Though other types of food *are* available, the idea of going to Japantown and not eating Japanese food seems positively un-American. **Mifune** (Kintetsu Bldg., 1737 Post St., Japan Center, tel. 415/922–0337) has tasty, inexpensive noodle dishes, including children's plates. At **Isobune Sushi** (Kintetsu Bldg., 1737 Post St., Japan Center, tel. 415/563–1030), you can pluck the sushi of your choice from little boats as they float around the counter, but every piece that's plucked must be paid for, so make sure your kids choose only what they can eat.

KEEP IN MIND Japantown is a relatively small area, bordered to the north by über-upscale Pacific Heights and to the south by the crime-ridden, public-housing-project-dense Western Addition. If you want to explore the area further, head north up Fillmore to the tempting eateries, chic boutiques, and artisan bakeries of Pacific Heights.

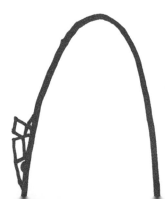

LAKE MERCED

37

Until sand dunes severed its narrow link to the Pacific about a century ago, this pretty lake in the far southwestern corner of San Francisco was an ocean-side lagoon. Freshwater has replaced saltwater, and Lake Merced now serves as an emergency city reservoir. But it was long known as a recreational mecca, once providing some of the best and most accessible fishing, boating, picnicking, bicycling, and running in the city. These days the lake is in limbo: without a boat-rental concessionaire, it remains popular among trout anglers who fish from the shore. One of San Francisco's top public golf courses, tree-shaded Harding Park, lies along its shores.

Lake Merced has 7 miles of shoreline, bordered much of the way by tule rushes and frequented by migratory birds. A moderately level path that's a favorite of cyclists, skaters, runners, and walkers loops around the lake. The path is partly shaded by eucalyptus, cypress, and pine trees; wildflowers, ferns, and berry bushes also line the route.

EATS FOR KIDS Picnic tables and barbecue grills are situated around the lake. If you didn't bring your own supplies, your best bet is to head up to the restaurants on Sloat Boulevard.

MAKE THE MOST OF YOUR TIME Despite the questionable state of fishing at the lake these days, it remains popular first and foremost as a jogging site. Bring the kids here on a sunny day for some low-key hanging out with a view, and bring a pair of binoculars to check out the many species of birds that call the lake home. No permit is required to fish here.

A narrow isthmus cuts the lake almost in two, with the larger southern portion more popular for boating (bring your own). On the road to recovery after nearby construction caused the water level to drop alarmingly in the 1990s, the waters here continue to be stocked with trout. In fact, the lake was long one of the top spots for year-round fishing in the Bay Area, known for introducing countless young people to the sport. One of the best times to bring kids to the lake is Trout Day (www.caltroutday.org), held each fall. Kids can watch casting demonstrations, then borrow rods for free and fish in youth-only area stocked with rainbow trout. They'll also learn about watershed conservation in a place that embodies the importance of working to preserve the natural resources right under our noses.

If you like this sight you may also like Golden Gate Park (#41), the Presidio (#17), and Tilden Park (#6).

KEEP IN MIND A few years ago, the boathouse that rented boats and fishing supplies to visitors here closed down. Oversight of the recreation area itself has changed hands from the parks department to the Public Utilities Commission. The PUC has preliminary plans to reopen the boathouse as a recreation facility, possibly with boat rental, but nothing is likely to happen before at least 2009. If you'd rather get out on the lake than play around it, stay tuned for details.

Loaded with interactive exhibits geared toward children and good for hours of entertainment, this is the East Bay's version of San Francisco's Exploratorium. Big hands-on displays and flashy special exhibitions are typical here, with an emphasis on biology, chemistry, and astronomy. Nestled on a winding road high in the Berkeley hills, this museum was built as a memorial to Ernest O. Lawrence, the University of California at Berkeley's first Nobel prize–winning laureate and an inventor of the atomic bomb.

Inside, head straight for whatever temporary exhibit is on; whether it's walking a tightrope high above the ground or using a hydrophone to listen for whale sounds underwater, these exciting shows keep kids busy for a good while. The permanent exhibits appeal to different age ranges. Older kids dig the nanoZone, where they can explore the science of the smallest things there are—nanotechnology—through computer games and a simulated scanning electron microscope. In the Real Astronomy Experience, older kids can measure a planet and track an asteroid's path. At the Idea Lab, the 5–8 crowd makes paper copters and hoop gliders,

MAKE THE MOST OF YOUR TIME When the skies are clear on the first and third Saturday evening of each month, you can stargaze with your family; hours are April–mid-September 9–11 and mid-September–March 8–10 (even though the museum is closed). Astronomers bring their telescopes to give interested visitors a free peek at the moon, planets, star clusters, and galaxies. Call the hall and select the astronomy information option for tips on what constellations, eclipses, and such you and your kids can see in the sky on a particular night. If after visiting the museum the kids need some running space, nearby Tilden Park (#6) has miles of trails and lots of open space.

Centennial Dr. near
Grizzly Peak Blvd., Berkeley

510/642-5132;
www.lawrencehallofscience.org

 $9.50 adults, $7.50 youths 5–18,
$5.50 children 3–4; planetarium $3
adults, $2.50 ages 18 and under

 Daily 10–5

3 and up

experiments with super-strong magnets, and builds with Legos. The Earthquakes exhibit contains a working seismograph and tips on surviving the Big One. YEA! (Young Explorers Area), for preschoolers, has puppets, blocks, books, and an insect zoo.

Want to pet a snake or hold a tarantula? Head to the Biology Discovery Lab; along with computer labs, Holt Planetarium shows, films, lectures, and laboratory demonstrations, it's available only in summer or on weekends and holidays. (Most planetarium shows are for kids 8 and older, but there are special shows for ages 4 and up.) In addition, the museum hosts summer fun days—often Wednesday—where kids get to do cool stuff like make ice cream or walk with stilts, as well as family workshops and highly respected classes.

If you like this sight you may also like the California Academy of Sciences (#57).

KEEP IN MIND

LHS is renowned for its excellent programs for kids 4 years old and up. These last from 50 minutes to an entire week and cover everything from kitchen science and animal homes to Lego robotics and crime-fighting technology. If you're not able to take advantage of their on-site programs, definitely stop at the **Discovery Corner Store** (tel. 510/642–7771).

EATS FOR KIDS The museum's **Bay View Café** (tel. 510/486–1807) serves hot dogs, soups, sandwiches, and salads and has a section for those who bring their own food. You can also picnic at nearby Tilden Park or drive back down out of the hills to eat at **Fatapple's** (1346 Martin Luther King Jr., Way, tel. 510/526–2260), where the burgers always draw big crowds and summertime olallieberry shakes are legendary. Join the line at the **Cheese Board Pizza Collective** (1512 Shattuck Ave., 510/549–3055), which serves only one kind of vegetarian pizza each day—the best in town, whatever the toppings.

LEGION OF HONOR

One of the city's top fine-arts museums, the Legion of Honor is a showcase for European paintings, sculpture, tapestries, and furniture dating from medieval times. Works by the French Impressionists and the sculptor Auguste Rodin are highlights. Equally stunning is the gleaming palacelike structure itself, which was designed in 1924 in the style of the 18th-century Palais de Legion d'Honneur in Paris and intended as a memorial to California's World War I dead. Renovated in the 1990s, with a pyramidal glass skylight illuminating the new lower-level galleries, the museum occupies a splendid location in Lincoln Park, in the Richmond District. Rodin's famous sculpture *The Thinker,* made from an 1880 cast, sits just outside the front entrance.

Depending on the ages of your children, allow about an hour or two for a typical visit. Stick to the basics. Many school-age kids enjoy paintings by French Impressionists, and the museum has one of Monet's famous *Water Lilies*. Be sure to take them to the two Rodin galleries, too, which contain about 70 works by the French sculptor (see if they

KEEP IN MIND Although certainly worthwhile, the Legion of Honor is possibly the most staid museum in town and doesn't accommodate small children particularly well. If you have little ones with you, consider visiting on the weekend. The museum may be busier then, but it's also louder and easier to blend in with the crowd.

MAKE THE MOST OF YOUR TIME Wild and windswept Lincoln Park has 270 acres of greenery. At its eastern end, 200-foot-high cliffs offer dramatic views of the Golden Gate Bridge, and hiking trails lead off along the headlands. Perhaps the most beloved path in the city, the Land's End trail starts near the museum, at the end of El Camino del Mar, and follows the cliffs west all the way to the Cliff House. It's a gorgeous, newly restored trail, but parts can be dangerous, so keep small children close. The public Lincoln Park Golf Course (tel. 415/221–9911) is reasonably priced for its exceptional setting.

100 34th Ave., Lincoln Park (enter park at Clement St. and 34th Ave.)

 415/750–3600; www.thinker.org/legion

 $10 adults, $6 youths 13–17; $2 off with Muni transfer; 1st T free

 T–Su 9:30–5:15

 6 and up

can spot the one called *Mask of a Woman with a Turned-Up Nose*). And if your kids haven't been exposed to much European art, they can see their first examples of Peter Paul Rubens and Rembrandt here.

On most Saturday afternoons at 2, you can take part in one of the special 1½-hour, drop-in programs the museum offers for kids and their parents, both of which include gallery tours and art classes. Kids ages 7–12 can attend Doing and Viewing Art, while younger art aficionados (ages 4–6) get their own chance to see and try their hands at art in Big Kids, Little Kids (parental accompaniment required for this one). The programs are free with paid museum admission, but call ahead (tel. 415/750–3658) to make sure they are offered the day you come. They're a great way to introduce even preschoolers to the world of art, and your kids might just surprise you with their enthusiasm.

If you like this sight you may also like the San Francisco Museum of Modern Art (#12).

EATS FOR KIDS The museum's attractive **Legion of Honor Cafe** (tel. 415/750–7639) offers Pacific views along with good sandwiches and salads. Weekend lunch lines can get brutal, though, so it's often quicker (and cheaper) to eat elsewhere. Local favorite **Bill's Place** (2315 Clement St., tel. 415/221–5262) is known for its juicy burgers and patio dining. Families flock to the outstanding dim sum and other Chinese food at **Ton Kiang** (5821 Geary Blvd., tel. 415/752–4440), so get here early, especially on weekends.

LIBERTY SHIP JEREMIAH O'BRIEN

Approach this hulking ship and you'll feel smaller and smaller. Then climb aboard to get a sense of the vastness of this floating city, built in a 40-day wartime frenzy. During World War II, some two-thirds of America's fleet of more than 2,700 Liberty Ships were built in the Bay Area. (The Liberty Ships were part of a merchant fleet designed to carry troops and wartime supplies including tanks and planes across the oceans and took part in landings ranging from Normandy to Guadalcanal.) Ironically, the U.S.S. *Jeremiah O'Brien* was built in Oregon. But more than a half century later, the *Jeremiah O'Brien*—the only Liberty Ship to remain afloat and in its original condition—is now integrally associated with San Francisco, berthed at Pier 45 at Fisherman's Wharf.

The city, and the entire area, embraced the gray-hulled ship and its history when, in 1994, it was restored and sailed by volunteers across the Atlantic to mark the 50th anniversary of D-Day, for which it had ferried troops. In fact, it was the only U.S. vessel to both take part in the Normandy invasion and return for the anniversary.

MAKE THE MOST OF YOUR TIME If you think the *Jeremiah O'Brien* feels claustrophobic, visit another authentic World War II vessel anchored at Pier 45, this one a restored submarine. Launched in 1943, the U.S.S. *Pampanito* (tel. 415/775-1943) saw action in the Pacific, sank six enemy warships, and rescued 73 allied POWs. Self-guided audio tours lead through the cramped crew's and officers' quarters, the engine rooms, and the torpedo room. Admission is $9 for ages 13 and up, $3 for children 6–12, and $20 for a family pass, which includes two adults and up to four kids under 18. It's open daily.

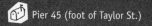 Pier 45 (foot of Taylor St.)

 $8 ages 15 and up, $4 children 6–14

 Daily 9–4

 415/544-0100; www.ssjeremiahobrien.org

6 and up

Today, the entire ship maintains its 1940s appearance. As you and your children walk the decks, it can be hard to imagine the tension the crew faced in open waters on their perilous journeys; the massive antiaircraft guns (no longer loaded, of course) on vigil serve as a stark reminder. Go below and you might feel like a rat in a maze as you explore the narrow, labyrinthine corridors, the sailors' quarters, the radio operator's room, and the bridge. It's a claustrophobic—for some, downright scary—experience to descend to the vessel's lower level and into the depths of the boiler room, where the enormous engines (which appeared in the movie *Titanic*) are still in working order. The engines are tuned up on "steaming weekends"—usually the third weekend of the month—when they're operated dockside.

If you like this sight you may also like the Hiller Aviation Museum (#40).

KEEP IN MIND
Visiting the *Jeremiah O'Brien* with small children can be harrowing; the ship is positively full of things to trip over and run into, and places to duck into. If you do bring little ones aboard, hang on to them! Or better yet, save this visit until it's safe to take your eyes off them.

EATS FOR KIDS For burgers, fries, and shakes, try **Johnny Rockets** (81 Jefferson St., tel. 415/693-9120). If you opt for takeout or have picnic supplies with you, head down the street to Aquatic Park or Victorian Park, at the cable-car turnaround.

LINDSAY WILDLIFE MUSEUM

33

ittle eyes grow wide with wonder as kids go toe to toe with animals like bobcats, foxes, bald eagles, and snakes, getting closer than they ever could in the wild, or even at the zoo. The centerpiece of this East Bay museum, founded in 1955, is the nation's oldest and one of its largest wildlife rehabilitation centers. People bring thousands of injured or orphaned animals to the Lindsay for treatment each year, including hawks, owls, coyotes, amphibians, squirrels, and rabbits. A bald eagle, for instance, may have become entangled in a power line. A coyote may have come to rely on humans for food. An owl may have flown into the path of a car. Nearly half are eventually returned to the wild. Those creatures too sick, injured, or tame to survive on their own may be put on display at this sparkling facility.

Don't think of the Lindsay as a zoo, though. Its goal is not to show off the animals but to teach the public about California wildlife, the impact of human activity on it, and how the needs of people can be balanced with those of wild animals. Daily presentations allow closer looks at certain animals, and you can watch as some are fed. But there's

KEEP IN MIND Also in Larkey Park, the Walnut Creek Model Railroad Society (2751 Buena Vista Ave., tel. 925/937–1888) has such an extravagant track layout that it's well worth scheduling your Lindsay visit to coincide with one of the few weekends the club runs the trains for visitors.

MAKE THE MOST OF YOUR TIME If you live locally and pay for a family membership ($65), your kids can use the Lindsay's Pet Library Program. This lets them check out a live domestic (not wild) rabbit, guinea pig, hamster, or rat for one week. These animals were once pets, but their former families couldn't keep them. It's a good way to find out if your kids are ready to have a pet full-time themselves or to just enjoy caring for one temporarily. Kids must be at least 6, and 10 for a rabbit.

Larkey Park, 1931 1st Ave., Walnut Creek

 $7 adults, $5 children 2–17

 Mid-June–Aug, W–Su 10–5; Sept–mid-June, Th–F 12–5, Sa–Su 10–5

 925/935–1978; www.wildlife-museum.org

2 and up

nothing flashy or cute here: The animals don't do tricks, you can't pet the wild creatures, and staff members don't pretend that the animals want to be here.

A number of exhibits are geared toward young children. In the Discovery Room, your youngsters can explore a scale model of a backyard that may be similar to your own and hunt for animals—an opossum, a squirrel, a screech owl, a bat, a raccoon—that make themselves at home here. The difference is that these animals aren't alive; they've visited the taxidermist. The Lindsay also offers a wide variety of rather pricey classes for all ages at the museum and beyond, some using live animals. But however you use the Lindsay, chances are your kids will come away with a greater understanding that wildlife protection begins at home.

If you like this sight you may also like the Randall Museum (#16) and the San Francisco Zoo (#11).

EATS FOR KIDS Larkey Park has picnic tables, and downtown Walnut Creek's North Main Street, about a mile from the museum, has many family-friendly eateries, including **Fuddruckers** (1940 N. Main St., tel. 925/943–1450), where burgers are king. For loaded, delicious pizza—including one rumored to induce labor—head to **Skipolini's Pizza** (1535 Giammona Dr., tel. 925/280–1100), just off North Main.

LOMBARD STREET

Officially, it's the 1000 block of Lombard Street, but everybody knows it as "the Crookedest Street in the World." (The end of Vermont Street on Potrero Hill may actually be *more* crooked, but it's way off the beaten path.) Lombard's eight hairpin curves, which zigzag down the east face of Russian Hill, are some of the most heavily driven, and photographed, stretches of roadway in existence.

To best appreciate Lombard Street, you'll need a car. At the intersection of Hyde and Lombard—where you may well encounter a mini–traffic jam—begin your snakelike drive down the red-cobblestone–lined street. It's impossible, really, to take it anything but slow or (for the driver) to do anything but steer back and forth. Kids usually love the ride. Have them count the curves as you go down, and to make it a real surprise, don't tell them where they're going before starting down. Chances are your car will show up in countless other people's photographs as you'll probably see scads of picture-snapping tourists both at the beginning and the end of the block.

MAKE THE MOST OF YOUR TIME Don't try this drive with an RV or any extra-long vehicle. If you don't have a car, you can ride a Powell-Hyde cable car to Lombard Street (ask the conductor to call out the nearest stop), and enjoy the scene as a pedestrian.

Lombard St. between Hyde and Leavenworth Sts.

 Free

415/974-6900 (San Francisco Convention and Visitor's Bureau)

Daily 24 hrs

4 and up

Once you've completed the driving portion, you may want to find a nearby parking space (admittedly easier said than done) to get a more leisurely view as a pedestrian. You can walk straight up or down the Crookedest Street—steps line either side of it—or just plant yourself at the top or bottom to see the procession of cars.

Designed with hairpin curves in the 1920s to enable drivers to negotiate the 40% grade, this block of Lombard is beautifully landscaped with flowers, shrubs, and other plants and lined on either side with houses, whose occupants must feel they're living in a fishbowl without the water.

If you like this sight you may also like the Filbert Steps (eastern face of Telegraph Hill, running from Coit Tower to Sansome Street) and Macondray Lane (between Jones and Taylor Sts. and Union and Green Sts., Russian Hill neighborhood).

KEEP IN MIND
Driving Lombard is fun because of the switchbacks, but to give the kids the ride of their lives, head a couple blocks south to Filbert Street. With a 31.5% grade, it's the steepest street in the city, so steep that when you cross Hyde, you can't see the street before your car. Most kids shriek appreciatively.

EATS FOR KIDS **Caffè Sapore** (790 Lombard St., tel. 415/474-1222), a few blocks down the hill, serves up hot and cold sandwiches, salads, soups, and pastries, and you can sit outdoors on nice days. **Zarzuela** (2000 Hyde St., tel. 415/346-0800), a white-tablecloth restaurant two blocks from the Crookedest Street, serves some of the city's best tapas (Spanish-style appetizer plates). The portions are perfect for kids, the sangria is top-notch, and service is friendly. **Swensen's Ice Cream** (1999 Hyde St., tel. 415/775-6818), across from Zarzuela, is the place to stop for an ice-cream cone, dispensing dozens of flavors daily.

MARIN HEADLANDS

S pread out just across the Golden Gate Bridge in stark, pastoral contrast to urban San Francisco, the Marin Headlands' 12,000 acres of rolling coastal hills stretch from East Ft. Baker to the rocky Pacific shores, offering a glorious natural getaway just minutes from town. The headlands contain more than 100 miles of paved roads, unpaved fire roads, and foot, mountain-bike, and horse trails, but to get your bearings, start on scenic Conzelman Road. Accessible from the northern end of the bridge, Conzelman Road hugs the cliffs for 5 miles to Point Bonita, where a ½-mile hike—steep in parts—leads to the 1855 Point Bonita Lighthouse, still in operation.

Along the way, you may want to stop and explore some old military fortifications and gun batteries. The tunnels and bunkers, which date from the 1870s, were constructed to help guard the Golden Gate from foreign attack. Battery 129, at Hawk Hill along Conzelman Road, provides unobstructed 360-degree views of the bridge, the city, and the bay. Kids often enjoy exploring its tunnels, originally designed for cannons. (Bring flashlights

EATS FOR KIDS There are no restaurants in the Marin Headlands, so bring a picnic lunch and find a hillside or beach with a view. In nearby Sausalito, **Hamburgers** (737 Bridgeway, tel. 415/332–9471) and **Scoma's** (588 Bridgeway, tel. 415/332–9551) are worthwhile.

MAKE THE MOST OF YOUR TIME Ft. Barry's onetime chapel has been converted to the Marin Headlands Visitor Center, which has displays on natural history and serves as the starting point for ranger-led walks. If you're interested in doing some camping or hiking here, call the visitor center or the Golden Gate National Recreation Area for information, directions, and trail conditions. One nice hike is the Tennessee Valley Trail, a relatively flat, 4-mile round-trip from the Tennessee Valley Road parking area to Tennessee Beach on the Pacific. With older kids, you could also try the 8-mile, round-trip hike to Muir Beach.

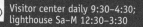
and old clothes.) Ft. Baker, at the foot of the bridge, now houses the Bay Area Discovery Museum (#61).

For many kids, the most memorable part of a trip to the headlands is a visit to the Marine Mammal Center (tel. 415/289–7325), open daily 10–4 and free, just above the beach at Ft. Cronkhite. This rescue and rehab center for sick, injured, or orphaned sea lions, seals, sea otters, whales, and porpoises is one of the world's largest wildlife hospitals. Here you can learn about ocean life, hear how marine biologists rescue whales stranded on nearby beaches, and, best of all, actually see some recuperating animals, perhaps seal pups being bottle-fed by volunteers. Not far beyond, Rodeo Lagoon is populated with loons, grebes, and other birds. Rodeo Beach lies just past the lagoon.

If you like this sight you may also like Año Nuevo State Reserve (#65), Point Reyes National Seashore (#18), and Mt. Tamalpais State Park (#27).

KEEP IN MIND If you're in the headlands on a September or October weekend—prime outdoor time in the Bay Area—plan a stop at Hawk Hill. You'll encounter dozens of folks ignoring the prime view, instead looking skyward. These are volunteers for the Golden Gate Raptor Observatory (tel. 415/331–0730), here to count the migrating peregrine falcons, golden eagles, ospreys, and more. Some extract birds from the netting the group sets up—it doesn't harm them—and in one swift move, band the birds for tracking purposes and send them on their way.

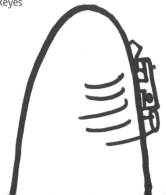

MARINA GREEN

Looking for a glorious grassy expanse to romp or relax on a luxuriantly sunny day? Well, okay, there are a few of those in the city. But if you want your park on the waterfront, with expansive views of the bay, fancy boats, and Alcatraz, close to some of the best kid spaces, in town, look no further. The Marina Green is one of San Francisco's prettiest parks, occupying a prime location along San Francisco Bay. Running the equivalent of eight city blocks, it's popular with kite-flyers, runners, in-line skaters, bicyclists, jugglers, sunbathers, picnickers, and touch-football and volleyball players. It's a short walk from the beach at Crissy Field, which is part of the Presidio (#17), and borders the Marina Small Craft Harbor, where hundreds of pleasure boats are docked. Its western end is across from one of the country's top family museums, the Exploratorium (#47).

This is one of San Francisco's top spots for kite-flying. On weekends you may see dozens of colorful, elaborate kites—some shaped like dragons, butterflies, or other exotic

MAKE THE MOST OF YOUR TIME Just east of the Marina Green sits Ft. Mason Center (tel. 415/441–3400; www.fortmason.org), a former military post that's now a cultural center containing the Young Performers Theatre (tel. 415/346–5550), where kids are the stars; the Children's Art Center (tel. 415/771–0292), which holds open art classes Monday–Saturday for kids 2–12; fun browsing at the Friends of the SF Public Library store (Bldg. D, tel. 415/771–3777); and some small galleries, including the Museo Italo Ameri-cano (tel. 415/673–2200) and the SFMOMA Artists Gallery (Bldg. A, tel. 415/441–4777). Except where otherwise noted, all are in Building C.

creatures—with long tails flapping in the breezes. Big flat expanses and a regular breeze off the bay usually make flying good for everyone.

With a small detour, you can catch one of San Francisco's most unusual—and overlooked—attractions, at the eastern tip of the breakwater that forms the Marina Small Craft Harbor. Start on the western end of the Marina Green (at the foot of Baker Street); then follow the path past the St. Francis Yacht Club—boat-loving kids will move slowly here—east to the Wave Organ. Here "natural music" is made by waves as they funnel through some 20 granite pipes. Come at high tide for the best effect. Your kids can climb on the rocks while you relax on the stone steps and enjoy the "concert" along with views of yachts and the bay. Even if this is as close as you'll ever get to a yacht, it's a million-dollar experience.

If you like this sight you may also like Golden Gate Park (#41).

EATS FOR KIDS **Greens to Go** (Ft. Mason Center, Bldg. A, tel. 415/ 771–6330) is a take-out stand at **Greens** vegetarian restaurant, where you can get sandwiches, salads, and baked goods for picnicking at Marina Green. The friendly folks at **Los Hermanos Mexican Food** (2026 Chestnut St., tel. 415/921–5790) serve great tacos, burritos stuffed to bursting, and other Mexican standbys in their tiny storefront.

KEEP IN MIND From Marina Green, face south (away from the water) and look toward the neatly kept houses lining Marina Boulevard. Imagine that you're standing here in October 1989, when a powerful earthquake severely damaged the Marina District. Many houses, streets, and sidewalks crumbled from the enormous waves of energy that traveled all the way from Santa Cruz.

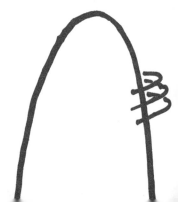

MISSION CLIFFS

When you walk in and stand face-to-face with a five-story climbing wall, you may think, "Huh?" But strap harnesses on the kids and watch 'em go. San Francisco's only indoor rock-climbing gym, one of the largest in the Bay Area, is the place to get your family psyched for tackling the granite cliffs or massive boulders of Yosemite—or at least that big rock in your backyard. Within a giant former warehouse in the Mission District, Mission Cliffs offers 14,000 square feet of artificial climbing terrain with a 50-foot-high lead wall and 2,000 square feet of bouldering "landscape."

Before your family can climb, a parent will need to take a Belay Safety Class ("belay" means securing the rope for a rock climber); it's $28 and includes a day pass and equipment rental. Recommended for first-time climbers, this class demonstrates the proper use of belay equipment, knot tying, and basic top-rope climbing. Kids climb brown walls studded with foot- and handholds and are secured by harness and rope to the ceiling or the top of the wall. If the kids like what they see, they can sign up for 10-week classes.

KEEP IN MIND If your kids are agile little monkeys under 10 or so, do yourself a favor and take the belay class (and climb a bit yourself) before you bring the little ones. It's torturous to watch other people scamper up the wall when you can only watch.

EATS FOR KIDS La Taqueria (2889 Mission St., tel. 415/285–7117) serves up terrific burritos, tacos, and fresh fruit drinks amid clean, colorful surroundings. The **St. Francis Fountain and Candy Store** (2801 24th St., tel. 415/826–4200), the city's oldest (1918) and most atmospheric soda fountain, is famous for its ice-cream treats and candy, but also offers basic lunches and dinners.

 2295 Harrison St.

 415/550-0515;
www.mission-cliffs.com

 $10–$16 adults, $10 children
under 14; equipment rentals $5

 M–F 6:30 AM–10 PM, Sa–Su 9–7

 6 and up

Kids can take private lessons ($35 an hour for one child, $60 for two) with one-on-one instruction. Another popular offering is group birthday parties, which include two hours of supervised climbing ($100 for up to 5 kids, plus $20 for each additional child). Weekly summer camps are offered, too. Instruction not only teaches your children about climbing but also should help them develop balance, coordination, concentration, and self-confidence. Though the atmosphere is informal and fun, supervision is close. Memberships provide discounts on lessons.

With lessons under their harness, most children learn the basics quickly. Many 7–9 year-olds grasp within a week how to put on a harness, tie a knot, belay, and climb. Younger kids generally take longer, but those 10 and up often learn in a lesson or two.

If you like this sight you may also like the Marin Headlands (#31).

MAKE THE MOST OF YOUR TIME Rock climb-
ing does pose physical risk, and everyone participating must sign a release of liability and assumption of risk form (a parent must sign for kids). If you have a strong feeling that your kids are going to want to climb, contact the gym first to be sure there's a belay class available, since staff can't belay walk-ins. Day passes are cheaper and the climbing less crowded before 3 PM.

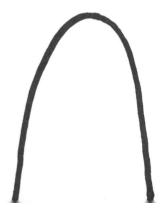

MISSION DOLORES

Historic buildings may not top your kids' lists of "fun things to do," but Mission Dolores has some things going for it. For starters, you can tell them it's the oldest building in San Francisco—more than 200 years old, in fact. The mission was completed in 1791, one of a string of 21 Spanish missions in California founded by Father Junipero Serra around the time the United States was gaining independence from England back on the East Coast.

Don't mistake the humble historic mission for the newer (1913), multidomed basilica next door, where most local parishioners come to worship. The old mission is small—the simplest, by design, of the state's historic missions. It's also one of the best preserved. Be sure your kids look up at the ceiling, where local Costanoans hand-painted Native American designs with vegetable dyes. The tiny chapel is decorated with frescoes and a hand-painted wooden altar; some artifacts were brought from Mexico by mule in the late 18th century. A small museum holds other historic pieces. You can rent an audio tour, which contains interesting background information, but it lasts 45 minutes, so it's best suited for older kids.

MAKE THE MOST OF YOUR TIME A visit to Mission Dolores can

be pretty quick, so you might want to combine a stop here with a tour of the Mission Murals (#25). For the young and the restless, Mission Dolores Park (18th and Dolores Sts.) is two blocks away. Here you'll find lots of green grass for picnicking and sunbathing, tennis and basket-ball courts, a playground, a dog-run area, and some great views of the city from its hillsides. If you need a pick-me-up, swing by **Tartine Bakery** (600 Guerrero St., tel. 415/487–2600) for outrageous pastries and good coffee in a trendy, Parisian atmosphere, or stop for fantastic ice cream at **Bi-Rite Creamery** (3692 18th St., tel. 415/626–5600).

 16th and Dolores Sts.

 $5 donation suggested, audio tour $7

415/621–8203
www.missiondolores.org

Daily 9–4

8 and up

The old cemetery next to the chapel is the most intriguing sight. Here in the oldest tombs in the city, dozens of early San Francisco pioneers and settlers are buried, including a number of children who died during the Gold Rush days—a poignant reminder of the hardships of those times. Lying in unmarked graves in back are the remains of an estimated 5,000 Native Americans. The cemetery also contains the burial sites of Don Francisco de Haro, the first mayor of San Francisco, and Don Luis Antonio Arguello, the first governor of Alta (or "upper") California, back in the days before California was part of the United States. But it was made famous by a scene in the 1958 Hitchcock film *Vertigo*, in which Kim Novak's character paid a visit here. It's still worth making a trip.

If you like this sight you may also like Angel Island State Park (#66) and the Presidio (#17).

KEEP IN MIND
This area is full of fun shopping. Paxton Gate (824 Valencia St., tel. 415/824–1872) is chockablock with natural science wonders like coyote skulls. Next door, 826 Valencia's Pirate Supply Store (826 Valencia St., tel. 415/642–5905) sells eye patches and glass eyeballs.

EATS FOR KIDS Picnic at Mission Dolores Park, or choose one of the area's inexpensive ethnic restaurants. **Pancho Villa Taqueria** (3071 16th St., tel. 415/864–8840) has some of the best burritos in the city and a large fresh-salsa bar. A block away, **Ti Couz** (3108 16th St., tel. 415/252–7373) specializes in Breton-style crepes, both savory (salmon, mushroom) and sweet (chocolate or fruit filled). Frequent lines at both restaurants, reflecting their popularity, are a potential downside, and the area can get a little dicey at night.

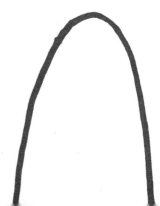

MT. TAMALPAIS STATE PARK

Usually called Mt. Tam, Mt. Tamalpais dominates the skyline in Marin County (rising to 2,571 feet) and is the top hiking and mountain-biking spot in the Bay Area. Dozens of trails lead to redwoods, waterfalls, and panoramic views stretching to San Francisco, Marin County, the bay, and the Pacific Ocean. About 50 of Mt. Tam's 200 miles of trails are within the 6,300-acre Mt. Tamalpais State Park, which occupies much of the mountain's western and southern slopes. Much of the rest of Mt. Tam lies within the boundaries of the Marin Municipal Water District and the Golden Gate National Recreation Area.

Make your first stop the small visitor center at the East Peak; here you can gather park information about hiking and learn about the park's nature. With young kids take the short, easy Verna Dunshee Trail, which loops around East Peak, the highest of Mt. Tam's three peaks. (The steep Plankwalk Trail then climbs ¼ mile to the top.) Another easy hike, the Mountain Theater Trail, leads from the Rock Spring parking area to a picnic area just below the Mountain Theater, where you can watch stage shows on weekends in May

KEEP IN MIND Camping at Mt. Tam is some of the most breathtaking in the Bay Area, and unfortunately, it's no secret. Especially if you want a cabin anytime during the dry season, you'll need to reserve months in advance.

MAKE THE MOST OF YOUR TIME Weather can play a big role in your enjoyment of Mt. Tam and may vary widely on the mountain itself: It's easy to go from warm sun into cool fog. The southern and western slopes, especially, are often fog-covered from June through August, and the best chance for clear skies and views is in late spring and fall, though winter also produces its share of crystal clear days. Most rain falls between November and April. Spring wildflower season is at its peak from March until mid-May, and yellow jackets may plague picnic areas in summer. Remember the Bay Area's motto: dress in layers.

and June; tickets go quickly. With energetic kids ages 10 and up, consider expanding your hiking to the redwood-lined Steep Ravine Trail, which drops 1,100 feet; the grueling Dipsea Trail, 6.8 miles one-way, site of a famous annual footrace; or the Matt Davis Trail, 6.7 miles one-way, which leads across the mountain toward Stinson Beach, a tiny, very mellow beach town with pretty good restaurants, cafés, and shops. Mountain bikes aren't permitted on foot trails, but they are allowed on fire roads, paved roads, and "grades." Mt. Tam has two campgrounds, Pantoll and Steep Ravine. The Pantoll Campground lies between the mountain summit and Muir Woods and has 16 walk-in tent sites ($15 per night), awarded at the Pantoll ranger station on a first-come, first-served basis. The Steep Ravine Environmental Campground, on an ocean bluff south of Stinson Beach, has 10 rustic cabins ($75 a night) and seven tent sites ($15). Parking permits and reservations are required year-round.

If you like this sight you may also like the Marin Headlands (#31).

EATS FOR KIDS Picnic tables are available at Rock Spring, Bootjack, Laurel Dell Meadow, and the East Peak summit, which also has a **snack bar.** Get seafood and good burgers at the **Sand Dollar** (3458 Shoreline Hwy., tel. 415/868–0434), home of Stinson Beach's most enticing patio since 1921.

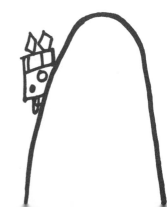

MUIR WOODS NATIONAL MONUMENT

Snuggled in a cool, often foggy redwood-lined canyon on the southeastern lower slopes of Mt. Tamalpais, 12 miles north of the Golden Gate Bridge, Muir Woods National Monument is the world's most famous stand of old-growth redwoods—the last remnants of soaring trees that once covered the mountain and many parts of the Bay Area. As California's most-visited redwood park (more than 1 million visitors a year), this is definitely nature for the masses: The main hiking trails are paved, and the woods are a regular stop on tour bus excursions. But the virgin redwoods—accented with green ferns and colorful azaleas, the scents of moss and bay, and the sounds of splashing Redwood Creek—are so majestic that tranquillity still seems to prevail. You won't find the tallest redwoods here—those are farther north—but the trees in Muir Woods are up to 250 feet tall.

Six miles of trails lie fully within the 560-acre park, and several can be negotiated by kids of just about any age. The 2 miles of paved trails along the canyon floor are mostly level and suited for strollers, and four bridges spanning Redwood Creek allow you to make short

MAKE THE MOST OF YOUR TIME A few tips can help avoid disappointment or discomfort while visiting Muir Woods: Arrive by midmorning or in late afternoon to avoid the crush of visitors, and go midweek if possible. (Parking lots, including the overflow lots, often fill up.) Roads to the park are steep and winding, and long trailers are prohibited. Bring jackets or sweatshirts; redwoods flourish in cool, foggy climates, and this is one of them. Watch for poison oak and stinging nettles just off the trails. Better yet, stay on the trails. Although camping isn't permitted here, you can camp in adjacent Mt. Tamalpais State Park.

loops. The tallest trees in the park are found along the Main Trail in Bohemian Grove (a ½-mile loop from the parking lot) and in Cathedral Grove (a 1-mile loop). With school-age kids, venture just a bit farther, along the unpaved trails—such as the Ben Johnson Trail (2½ miles round-trip)—that lead up out of the canyon into Mt. Tamalpais State Park (#27), and you'll be surprised at how few other folks you'll meet.

If your kids are around ages 6–12, pick up a Junior Ranger activity book, full of bits about the nature in the woods and activities like crossword puzzles. But whatever their age, children will probably spend at least some time just gaping in wonder at the awesome natural giants around them.

If you like this sight you may also like Golden Gate Park (#41).

EATS FOR KIDS

A **café** near the main entrance serves burgers, hot dogs, and apple pie. Picnicking isn't permitted in Muir Woods but is allowed in nearby Muir Beach and adjacent Mt. Tamalpais State Park. See the latter for information on picnicking and area restaurants.

KEEP IN MIND Nestled among the trees, hidden from view from the road, is the Swiss-style chalet Naturfreundehaus (30 Ridge Ave., Mill Valley, tel. 415/388–9987). Part of an Austrian nature and hiking club, the lodge has a huge porch with fantastic forest views. On weekends and during its annual festivals—in May, July, and September—you can choose from a large selection of German beer and dig into some traditional food (think sausage) while watching folks in lederhosen and dirndl spin on the dance floor. Despite the imbibing and oompah sounds, plenty of folks bring their kids for a little culture among the trees.

MURALS OF THE MISSION DISTRICT

They're some of the city's least-known artistic treasures—possibly more famous in Europe than in San Francisco—and you don't need to visit a museum to see them. All you have to do is take a walk (or a bike ride or a drive). Hundreds of outdoor murals decorate the Mission District, and their often brilliant colors and bold subjects captivate kids.

The first—and still best-known—group of murals is in little Balmy Alley (24th to 25th St. between Harrison and Treat Sts.). Back in the early 1970s, community artists—both adults and children, working alone or in groups—started to adorn the block-long byway's walls with murals featuring such themes as peace in Central America, Latino heritage, and neighborhood pride. (The Mission District is heavily Hispanic.) Since then, dozens more muralists have joined in, so that today much of the street, including walls, fences, and garage doors, is covered with artwork.

KEEP IN MIND Parts of the Mission—including the area south of Balmy Alley—can be sketchy. Since mural-viewing is obviously a daytime activity, you shouldn't have any problems, but you'll want to head out of here, at least farther west into the Mission, before dark.

Like those in Balmy Alley, most Mission District murals are in the area bordered on the west by Mission Street, the east by Potrero Avenue, the north by 20th Street, and the

MAKE THE MOST OF YOUR TIME With small children, combine art and play at the 24th Street Minipark (24th and Bryant), where murals cover the walls that surround the park and the littles can climb on a gorgeous, mosaic-covered Quetzalcoatl serpent that plunges into and rises from the ground. In addition to the tours conducted through the Precita Eyes Mural Arts and Visitors Center, less frequent—but free—walking tours of the Mission murals are offered by City Guides (tel. 415/557–4266). These tours are given only on selected Saturdays, so call for a schedule.

south by Precita Avenue, next to Precita Park. Down the block from Balmy Alley, Precita Eyes Mural Arts and Visitors Center sells Mission mural walk maps for $3.95, allowing you to take your own self-guided tour any time you like.

You can also take a guided walking tour. They are best for children 10 and older who are particularly interested in art, but all ages are welcome. Use your best judgment. Precita Eyes offers the most frequent walking tours, which last 1½–2 hours and cover a six- to eight-block area with 75–90 murals. Drop-in tours are given on weekends; call for reservations for other days. A ½-hour slide show on the making of murals precedes the afternoon tour. Tour guides—muralists themselves—are attuned to the needs of kids. For any walk wear comfortable shoes, and carry snacks and water.

If you like this sight you may also like Coit Tower (#50).

EATS FOR KIDS Restaurants with a heavy emphasis on Mexican and Latin American food line 24th Street. One, **Roosevelt Tamale Parlor** (2817 24th St., tel. 415/550–9213), has been dishing up Tex-Mex classics since 1922. **La Victoria Mexican Bakery** (2937 24th St., tel. 415/550–9292), where you can buy Mexican-style pastries, is another longtime favorite.

NOB HILL

Nob Hill, which rises steeply to a height of 376 feet above Chinatown and the Financial District, has been one of the city's most prestigious addresses since the late 19th century, when cable cars finally conquered the hill and railroad magnates and Comstock Lode silver barons built the most expensive homes California had ever seen here. All but one of the houses were destroyed in the 1906 earthquake, and the lone survivor, the brownstone Flood Mansion, is now the ultra-exclusive Pacific Union Club. But the legacy of the "Big Four" railroad magnates—Charles Crocker, Mark Hopkins, Collis P. Huntington, and Leland Stanford—and other tycoons lives on in the luxury apartment buildings and hotels (including the Mark Hopkins, Huntington, and Fairmont) that line this high-rent hill. To rub elbows with the wealthy—or, at least, their dogs, kids, and nannies—take a break at the top of the hill in neat, tidy Huntington Park. Find a spot on a bench while your kids take to the swings, slide, and climbing structures on the small, sand-based playground.

MAKE THE MOST OF YOUR TIME Grab a cup of joe (or an iced tea for the kids) in the cathedral's basement café, serving Peet's Coffee; large, clean restrooms are downstairs as well. Part of the fun of visiting Nob Hill is riding the California Street cable-car line to the top. The ride is steep and as much fun as many theme park rides for kids. You can board the cable car anywhere along California Street between Van Ness Avenue and the foot of Market Street. Rides cost $5 each for anyone 6 or older; little ones are free. Considering the price, if you don't have an all-day cable-car pass or a Muni pass, you might want to combine your Nob Hill and Cable Car Museum visits.

California, Taylor, Sacramento, and Mason Sts.

 Free

🕐 Cathedral daily 7–6

☎ 415/831–2700 Huntington Park,
415/749–6300 Grace Cathedral

🍼 All ages, cathedral 10 and up

Across from the park towers gothic Grace Cathedral (Taylor and California Sts.), modeled after Notre Dame in Paris. The Episcopal cathedral has a 15th-century French altarpiece, luminous stained-glass windows, and gilded-bronze doors similar to Filippo Brunelleschi's Baptistery doors in Florence, Italy. So visiting here is like taking the kids on a minitrip to Europe. Keith Haring's metal triptych altarpiece—his last work—adorning the Interfaith AIDS Chapel inside adds a distinctly American touch. Don't overlook the cathedral's intriguing indoor and outdoor labyrinths, based on one at France's Chartres Cathedral. Each labyrinth forms a meandering path that leads in a geometric pattern to the center of a circle and back out again, representing an interfaith path of prayer and meditation. Though many children like to walk the labyrinths, they should respect others following the paths and not use them for racing.

If you like this sight you may also like Lombard Street (#32).

KEEP IN MIND
The last remaining cable-car signal tower in the city presides over the intersection of Powell and California streets, where the cable-car tracks cross. These streets are so steep that the cable-car drivers can't see one another approaching, so the person working the tower manually signals the cars to stop and go.

EATS FOR KIDS The **Nob Hill Café** (1152 Taylor St., tel. 415/776–6500) dishes up pastas, pizza, and chocolaty desserts in friendly, upscale surroundings best for older kids. With younger kids, you'll want to head down the hill, away from all the fancy places. You catch the Powell–Mason cable car at California and Powell and head down to Washington Street for good sandwiches and hefty quiche at **Gallery Café** (1200 Mason St., tel. 415/296–9932), just across the street from the Cable Car Museum (#58).

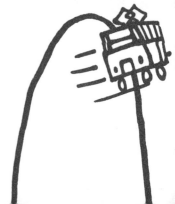

OAKLAND MUSEUM OF CALIFORNIA

Maybe because it's across San Francisco Bay in Oakland, this attractive, innovative museum on the south shore of Lake Merritt (#53 for lake activities) doesn't get the recognition it deserves. Its architecture alone—three tiers of galleries with gardens, courts, terraces, lawns, and pond in a complex covering four square blocks—makes it stand out.

Two permanent exhibits especially capture the imagination of kids. First, in the Natural Sciences Gallery, kids are greeted by a snarling wolverine and a big-eyed harbor seal, and they can search the exhibits for well-concealed animals as they walk through California's ecological systems. Here the film *Fast Flight* whisks viewers on a pulse-quickening trip over the state in five minutes. Then, in the Cowell Hall of California History, your kids can travel back to the days of Native Americans, missions and ranchos, the Gold Rush, the Victorian era, and 1960s-era California. Younger kids will want to head straight upstairs to ogle a collection of vintage vehicles, from a cherry-red "Mystery" car to a shining gold, red, and silver vintage fire engine that fought the flames in San Francisco after the 1906 quake.

KEEP IN MIND Even if you don't cover the whole museum, especially with younger children be sure to head outside to see the giant koi pond. For the little ones, a visit to the animals in the Natural Sciences Gallery and a gander at the Cowell Hall's vehicles followed by lunch in the café overlooking the pond is one very full day.

MAKE THE MOST OF YOUR TIME One especially fun time to visit the museum is during its Day of the Dead celebration, at the end of October or the beginning of November. Elaborate altars are on view, a *mercado* fills the plaza, and kids can paint sugar skulls and make other traditional crafts honoring those who have passed on. Oakland has another kid-friendly museum that's less known but well worth a visit: the Museum of Children's Art (538 9th St., tel. 510/465–8770), known as MOCHA. The two-floor museum displays art created by children, ranging from East Bay kids to those who live in other countries.

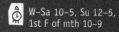

About once a month, the museum offers special events and workshops for families and kids, on subjects such as photography, dinosaurs, and box making. (Some are free; others require a materials fee.) Major temporary exhibits, covering such different topics as hot-rod culture and California caves, are displayed in the Great Hall, and the museum's courtyards often host open-air art exhibitions. It's enough to lure even die-hard San Franciscans over to the East Bay—an impressive feat in itself.

If you like this sight you may also like the California State Railroad Museum (#56), Ft. Point National Historic Site (#43), and the Wells Fargo History Museum (#3).

EATS FOR KIDS The museum's **OMCA Café** features hot en-
trées, sandwiches, soups, salads, snacks, and desserts, all fresh and reasonably
priced. Another option is to spread out a blanket under the shade trees along
the banks of Lake Merritt and have a picnic. Nearby **Zza's Trattoria** (552
Grand Ave., tel. 510/839–9124) is a child-friendly Italian restaurant.

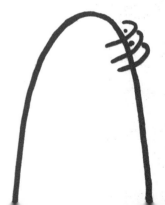

OAKLAND ZOO

Once known as one of the worst zoos in the country, with cramped and depressing animal enclosures, the Oakland Zoo now has facilities approaching those in some of the state's top zoos. High in the Oakland hills, it comprises 50 different exhibits on 100 acres within Knowland Park, harboring nearly 400 native and exotic animals.

Bright pink flamingos greet you in Flamingo Plaza, just inside the entrance; this makes a good orientation or meeting point. Straight ahead of Flamingo Plaza are the monkey, ape, and chimp habitats, perhaps the zoo's most interesting area. On especially lush, tropical Siamang Island and Gibbon Island, hooting primates swing through the trees in a rain-forest environment. Head off to the right for the African Veldt and Savanna areas, where giraffes, gazelles, lions, and elephants reside. The African Savanna, which simulates desert areas of eastern and southern Africa, is landscaped with man-made rocks, a waterfall, and Kikuyu-style "mud and cow dung" (actually disguised concrete) structures.

MAKE THE MOST OF YOUR TIME With smaller children, head
straight to the sprawling Valley Children's Zoo; with its running and climbing spaces, plus the fabulous bat and lemur exhibits, it's probably enough entertainment for little ones. In the regular zoo, the animal exhibits aren't fantastic, and older children may be finished quickly or disappointed. Though the zoo is normally open daily, it closes during bad weather. What's bad enough to make it close? If you're still in doubt after looking out the window, call the park to ask.

9777 Golf Links Rd. (off I-580), Knowland Park, Oakland

 510/632-9525; www.oaklandzoo.org

 $9.50 ages 15 and up, $6 children 2–14; parking $6

 Daily 10–4

All ages

To the left and rear is the wonderful Valley Children's Zoo (free with admission), where your kids can get closer to alligators than you ever thought possible. In the barnyard area, kids can pet and feed domestic sheep and pygmy goats. In the Rides Area, near the front, they can board a ⅔-size replica of a Civil War–era locomotive ($2). Look for the carousel, too, as well as some small carnival-type rides, but be sure to check the height limits to make sure your kids aren't too big. If they are, they may be ready for the Skyride ($2; open weekends only), a chairlift that provides a bird's-eye, 15-minute view of American bison and tule elk. The open cars go quite high, which might scare young kids.

If you like this sight you may also like the San Francisco Zoo (#11).

KEEP IN MIND
This is one hilly zoo, and getting around is quite a workout. If you feel like a sergeant at boot camp trying to urge your kids up yet another hill, consider renting a stroller near the front gate. Also: If you choose to drive here, you must park in the Zoo's lot.

EATS FOR KIDS This is one place where a picnic is the best on-site option: The zoo has lots of picnic tables in pleasant areas, and many of the eateries here only open on summer weekends. Outside the zoo, Knowland Park has plenty of grassy picnic areas with tables and barbecue facilities. The zoo's **Safari Café,** near the entrance, has standard concession food (read: unappetizing and overpriced) and some outdoor tables. The **food stand** in the Rides Area sells similar fare and is open summer weekends.

OCEAN BEACH

San Francisco's best-known beach is a wide, mostly flat, 4-mile blanket of sand that forms the western, Pacific Ocean edge of the city. Overseen by the National Park Service, Ocean Beach stretches south from the Cliff House to Ft. Funston (#44), which occupy cliffs overlooking it from opposite directions.

On the occasional warm, sunny day, the beach draws hundreds of sunbathers, Frisbee tossers, dog walkers, and kite-flyers taking advantage of the ocean breezes—and sometimes gusty winds. (This isn't Southern California, though, and since there are no lifeguard- or food stands to congregate around, the beach never feels crowded.) This is also a favored spot for watching the sunset. Some people never get out of their parked cars. Even on foggy, misty days—and there are many here—Ocean Beach is a gathering place for a diverse group of people in search of recreation. Anglers cast their lines for perch and stripers, and just below the Cliff House restaurant, expert surfers ride the waves. (This is not a place for beginners.) Because of the often rough, treacherous surf, swimming is dangerous; currents

KEEP IN MIND Ocean Beach has long been a favorite spot for summer bonfires, and with a dozen new fire rings—each designed and built by a local artist—the beach makes a more attractive all-day-and-into-the-night destination than ever.

MAKE THE MOST OF YOUR TIME The western edges of Golden Gate Park (#41) lie just across the highway from Ocean Beach. You can take your kids to see two historic windmills here. One, a restored 1902 Dutch windmill in the northwestern corner of the park, overlooks a tulip garden. The other, called the Murphy Windmill, was the world's largest when it was built in 1905, but has fallen into disrepair. Both once pumped water to the Strawberry Hill reservoir in the middle of the park.

Great Hwy. from Cliff House to Sloat Blvd.

 Free

Daily 24 hrs

 415/556–8642;
www.parksconservancy.org

All ages

are unpredictable, the undertow is strong, and there are no lifeguards. Besides, the water is downright cold. Watch kids carefully even if they're just playing along the shore.

One of the main draws of Ocean Beach runs right alongside it for the first mile or so down from the Cliff House: a broad paved pathway that attracts cyclists, rollerbladers, runners, walkers, and parents pushing strollers. Another pathway runs along the opposite side of the Great Highway, bordering Golden Gate Park, and remains paved all the way to Sloat Boulevard, about 3 miles away, where you can connect with the bike path around Lake Merced (#37). Because you'll ride on the road a bit toward the end, the latter portion of the bike route is suitable for older kids only.

If you like this sight you may also like China Beach (#52) and Limantour Beach at Point Reyes National Seashore (#18).

EATS FOR KIDS The **Beach Chalet** (1000 Great Hwy., tel. 415/ 386–8439), an often crowded brew pub, serves up buffalo wings, gumbo, and ocean views across the Great Highway from Ocean Beach; it's best for older kids. Your best bet is probably to bring your own food and have a picnic on the beach. Beach fires are permitted at times, but check with rangers about regulations beforehand.

PARAMOUNT'S GREAT AMERICA

Tackling 10 roller coasters and other daredevil rides at this movie- and TV-theme park is nothing less than a rite of passage for many Bay Area youngsters. Ten-year-olds who board the Vortex for a heart-thumping, stand-up roller-coaster ride know they're growing up; 12-year-olds who brave a 22-story, 91-feet-per-second, open-air fall on the Drop Zone can claim bragging rights all winter over those who held back.

Also for older, daredevil kids, Psycho Mouse takes you through 14 twists and hairpin turns. Top Gun, a jet coaster meant to simulate the sensation of flying an F-14 Tomcat jet fighter, provides short but intense thrills. As you catapult off into space at 50 mph, you experience a 360-degree vertical loop, two 270-degree "afterburn turns," and a "zero-gravity barrel roll." Another stomach-turner, Invertigo, takes riders forward and backward at 55 mph through a boomerang and vertical loop. Survivor: The Ride condenses the reality TV show into a rather odd but fun team competition, culminating in an outward facing, stomach-dropping spin on a giant disk.

MAKE THE MOST OF YOUR TIME
A few tips can help you get the most out of your visit. Note that most rides have minimum height requirements, and some of the kiddie rides have maximum height requirements (adults must be accompanied by kids). Explaining this to children of borderline height might ward off disappointment. If your kids plan to visit Boomerang Bay, Nickelodeon Central, or go on water rides, bring a change of clothing, or have them wear swimsuits. And if you plan to return soon, ask about upgrading to a WOW! card, good for unlimited repeat visits during the season; the more expensive VIP Pass includes parking ($10 a pop).

Great America Pkwy. between
U.S. 101 and Hwy. 237, Santa Clara

408/988-1776;
www1.cedarfair.com/greatamerica

$49.95 ages 3 and up
and over 48", $29.95
ages 3 and up and
under 48"

 Late Mar–mid-Oct, varying days (early
June–late Aug, daily) 10–varying hrs

 3 and up

Younger kids gravitate toward Nickelodeon Central—where they can meet Dora the Explorer and other favorites, ride gentle rides, and maybe even get slimed—and the adjacent KidZville, which has more than 20 rides and attractions. These include a mini–roller coaster, a little parachute drop, and the KidZconstruction play space, with room to romp and climb. The classic double-deck Carousel Columbia, near the park's front entrance, is the world's tallest. Great America also has the Grizzly, a classic wooden roller coaster, and three water rides.

For a quieter way to cool down, the park offers stage shows combining music, cartoon characters, and, in some cases, audience participation.

If you like this sight you may also like the Santa Cruz Beach Boardwalk (#10).

KEEP IN MIND
Although there's plenty here to entertain kids too young to appreciate the big rides, with the hefty cost of admission, parking, and food here, you might consider a cheaper option—like Children's Fairyland (#53), the Oakland Zoo (#22), or a community pool—and save the thrill of this park for those around 10 and up.

EATS FOR KIDS Needless to say, the food at the park is expensive and predictable. **Shaggy's Snack Shack,** in KidZville, has burgers and fries, as does the **American Café** in All American Corners. **The Outback Shack,** in Boomerang Bay, carries fish-and-chips, pizza, and salads. **Maggie Brown's,** in Hollywood Plaza, has chicken dinners. **Food Festival,** in County Fair, carries an assortment of sandwiches, pizza, hot dogs, and more. The park doesn't allow you to bring any food inside the gates but does provide a picnic area outside the main entrance.

PIER 39

This once-abandoned cargo pier on the eastern edge of Fisherman's Wharf (#45) was transformed into a waterside shopping and entertainment mall in the late 1970s, and it's been San Francisco's top tourist draw ever since. Publicists claim it's the country's most popular non-Disney attraction, and if you go at the height of tourist season, you probably won't dispute it.

Although many San Franciscans consider it a tacky tourist trap, local kids still head here in droves, alongside the out-of-towners. The good news is that it costs nothing to walk in and soak up the atmosphere and the bay views. For those, just follow the wooden boardwalks to the sides or rear of the pier. Rest assured, however, if you leave Pier 39 without lightening your wallet, you'll fall into the vast minority. More than 100 shops—including places to buy toys and candy—as well as eateries and entertainments line the double-deck pier. A double-decker, antique Venetian carousel entices younger children. Turbo Ride, a motion-simulated adventure ride, and a giant trampoline are popular with preteens

KEEP IN MIND Pier 39 can be overwhelming—for adults, let alone kids—and expensive. If your children start to show signs of sensory overload, hop on the F-line and ride a couple stops west toward Aquatic Park, where the sounds of lapping surf and the clang of the cable cars replaces the din of music and buskers.

MAKE THE MOST OF YOUR TIME Naturally, the sea lions don't have opening and closing hours, and you can watch them here any day of the week. However, to learn more about them, come for one of the free guided talks, offered some weekends by docents from Marin County's Marine Mammal Center (#31). The Marine Mammal Center also runs one of the pier's better stores (tel. 415/289–7373), selling clothing items, books, and gifts, with receipts benefiting that worthy cause.

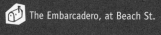 The Embarcadero, at Beach St.

 Free; some attractions charge

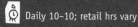 Daily 10–10; retail hrs vary

415/981–7437 recording,
415/705–5500 voice;
www.Pier39.com

 3 and up

and teens, who also flock to the video arcade. Other pier attractions include the Aquarium of the Bay (#64) and the Blue & Gold Fleet sightseeing ferries (#60).

Those with slender budgets and iron willpower, however, can spend enjoyable hours here with little cash outlay. Jugglers, magicians, and acrobats perform for loose change. But the best show may be a colony of California sea lions, which took up residence at the West Marina here in 1990 and have been delighting onlookers ever since. Their numbers vary depending on the season (winter is best, summer slimmest), but you may encounter anywhere from dozens to hundreds of the playful pinnipeds, who provide captivating displays of barking, frolicking, and jockeying for sunbathing position on the docks. And they don't even pass the hat at the end—at least, not yet.

If you like this sight you may also like Fisherman's Wharf (#45) and the Santa Cruz Beach Boardwalk (#10).

EATS FOR KIDS Pier 39 has about a dozen restaurants and is loaded with snack and sweets shops. One of the better ones is **Sea Lion Café** (tel. 415/434–2260), which serves fish-and-chips and overlooks the sea lions. The specialties at the **Boudin Sourdough Bakery & Café** (tel. 415/421–0185) are clam chowder and chili in a bread bowl, great on a cool, foggy day. The **Wipeout Bar and Grill** (tel. 415/986–5966) has a fun surf theme with a big kids' menu and outdoor as well as indoor tables.

POINT REYES NATIONAL SEASHORE

The Point Reyes peninsula encompasses 71,000 majestic acres of sheer natural wonder on the Marin County coast. You can hike to secluded beaches or through forests of pine and fir, view sea birds and tule elk, and drive through rugged, rolling grasslands.

You could easily spend a day just in the area around the large and inviting Bear Valley visitor center, the first site you reach after driving up the coast—especially appealing with younger kids. At the visitor center, kids can view stuffed versions of local wildlife and touch whale bones, and the rangers will recommend activities and trails specific to your needs and interests. Right outside, the intriguing, ½-mile-loop Earthquake Trail follows the San Andreas Fault near the epicenter of the famed 1906 San Francisco quake. A nearby ¼-mile trail leads to Kule Loklo, a replica of a Coast Miwok Indian village. At the Morgan Horse Ranch, learn how horses are trained for the National Park Service and maybe see a demonstration. The Bear Valley Trail, suited for many kids ages 5 and up, is an easy, 3-mile round-trip through a forest to a meadow and back; with older kids,

GETTING THERE Highway 1 up the coast is scenic, but it's also very slow and winding. You can reach Point Reyes from San Francisco in 90 minutes or less by taking U.S. 101 north to the San Anselmo exit. Turn left onto Sir Francis Drake Boulevard and stay on it all the way to the town of Olema. At the stoplight here, turn right onto Highway 1; then take a quick left onto Bear Valley Road, which leads to the visitor center about ½ mile farther north. Pick up a map here to find other park locations.

you can stretch it to an 8-mile round-trip leading to a string of secluded, golden-sand beaches.

If you're seeking easier beach access, head for Limantour Beach or Drakes Beach, both on sheltered Drakes Bay, where the water is usually calm but cold. Along a windswept, 15-mile stretch of Pacific Ocean are Point Reyes Beach North and South, where the surf is dangerous but the beachcombing great. In the northern reaches of the park, a 4-mile trail leads to spectacular Tomales Point and frequent sightings of tule elk; this hike is only for older kids with stamina. To reach Point Reyes Light, an 1870 lighthouse perched over the Pacific, you need to drive 22 scenic but winding miles from the Bear Valley visitor center and then climb down 300 steps to the lighthouse, which also means climbing 300 steps back up.

If you like this sight you may also like Año Nuevo State Reserve (#65).

KEEP IN MIND From around December to March, elephant seals come here to breed and birth their calves. You can view the seals anytime during that season from the Elephant Seal Overlook near Chimney Rock over Drakes Bay; on weekends docents share binoculars and their knowledge. Around New Year's to Easter, the areas around Chimney Rock and the lighthouse offer some of the best gray-whale viewing on the coast. From late April to early May, mothers and calves can often be spotted close to shore. Viewing areas can get so crowded during migration that a free shuttle runs on weekends from the Drakes Beach parking lot.

EATS FOR KIDS
Picnic at any beach. Drakes Beach even has a **snack bar** and picnic tables. Pick up supplies at **Perry's Delicatessen** (Sir Francis Drake Blvd., Inverness Park, tel. 415/663–1491). The **Station House Cafe** (Hwy. 1, Pt. Reyes Station, tel. 415/663–1515) has good sandwiches, salads, and patio dining.

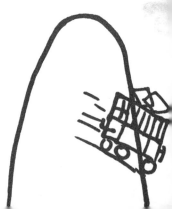

PRESIDIO NATIONAL PARK

Until fairly recently, this nearly 1,500-acre park overlooking the Golden Gate was a longtime military post. The Spanish came in 1776, establishing a walled fortification (or *presidio*) to protect the bay. After passing into Mexico's hands in 1822, the Presidio fell to the United States when California was acquired in 1846; it became the Sixth Army's base and a training ground for Civil War soldiers. In 1994 the Army moved out, and the Presidio became part of the Golden Gate National Recreation Area. Miles of bike routes and hiking trails wind along coastal bluffs, past hundreds of historic military buildings and defense installations, and over hills thick with cypress, eucalyptus, and pine trees. You can soak up some Presidio history at Ft. Point National Historic Site (#43), but the Presidio's real glory is its natural beauty. Pick up a hiking or bike trail map at the visitors center in the Officers' Club and strike out on your own—be sure to include at least one of the park's spectacular overlooks to view the bay or ocean—or check out the schedule (online or at the visitor center) and join a ranger-led tour.

KEEP IN MIND One Presidio oddity that kids usually appreciate is the Pet Cemetery, with leaning headstones and elaborate monuments bearing touching tributes to dogs, cats, rabbits—even a tortoise and iguana or two—who have passed on. See if you can find the oldest marker here: it dates to 1925.

MAKE THE MOST OF YOUR TIME There's so much to see and do in the Presidio that it's hard to know where to start, and winding roads can make finding certain locations a bit tricky. So stop in at the Presidio Visitors Information Center, which has maps, brochures, trail guides, and schedules for free, ranger-led guided walks and bike tours. On weekends, the ranger walks last from 45 minutes to three hours and cover the Presidio's natural history, the area's strategic military history, and the bay-side tidal zone. If you don't have a car, the free PresidiGo shuttle, which operates year-round, is a great way to get around.

Main gate, Lombard and Lyon Sts.; visitor center, Lincoln Blvd. and Montgomery St.

 Free

Visitor center daily 9–5, museum W–Su 12–4

 415/561–4323 visitor center; www.nps.gov/prsf

 All ages

Kids of all ages flock to Crissy Field, a restored marshland, beach, and parklike area along the bay east of the Golden Gate Bridge, and you could easily spend the day here, especially with small children. Families come to wade at a beach, watch windsurfers in the bay or birds in a tidal marsh, picnic, bike, skate, or fly kites. Two nature centers engage kids with sea creatures and hands-on activities, Baker Beach, a scenic stretch of sand west of the bridge, is popular for sunbathing but has dangerous surf. Some kids will get a kick out of an amble around George Lucas's Letterman Digital Arts Center, especially to find the Yoda fountain. The grounds are stunningly landscaped and open to the public.

In the park's southern reaches, Julius Kahn playground—with basketball and tennis courts, a softball field, and grass for picnics—has spectacular play structures, great for climbers and those who love to spin. Mountain Lake Park, also on its southern flanks, has a bi-level playground with fun play options for both younger and older kids.

If you like this sight you may also like Angel Island (#66).

EATS FOR KIDS The Presidio's picnic areas include tables at Crissy Field and barbecue facilities behind Baker Beach. The **Warming Hut** (W. Crissy Field Dr., tel. 415/561–3042) sells made-to-order sandwiches, soups, and snacks, and makes a mean cup of hot chocolate—perfect for those foggy days. You can eat indoors or at one of the picnic tables or on the grass outside. The café at the **Crissy Field Center** (603 Mason St., tel. 415/561–7690) serves darn good, often organic sandwiches and salads in a super kid-friendly atmosphere. They also have a kids' menu and make a mean cup of coffee.

RANDALL MUSEUM

This small children's museum run by the city's Recreation and Park Department is so far off the beaten path that it's a wonder anyone ever finds it. Yet savvy San Francisco parents know that its value far outweighs its size and out-of-the-way location. Set in Corona Heights Park, the Randall occupies a dramatic perch overlooking the city between the Haight-Ashbury and Castro districts. Inside, the museum is chock-full of intriguing hands-on exhibits in the realms of nature, art, and science.

Your children will find minerals to touch, dinosaur bones to peruse, and chemistry and biology labs to test out. An earthquake exhibit has a working seismograph, a demonstration of how the earth's shifting tectonic plates can cause quakes, and a fun area called Make-a-Quake, in which kids get to jump up and down to see how much "seismic force" they can produce themselves. In the live animal room, you'll probably hear a parent assure a child that those uncaged owls and hawks lurking high on the wall are stuffed, but be prepared to jump when an eye opens. These animals are injured and unable to live in the wild—or

MAKE THE MOST OF YOUR TIME Corona Heights Park (sometimes called Museum Hill or Red Rock) offers one of the great "hidden" overlooks of San Francisco. The views are a real bonus, especially for parents, but older kids often enjoy following the trails and the steep climb to the top of the rocks. The lure for young kids is a park and playground below the museum with swings and sand.

swoop down off the wall at you. Your children can learn about and get close-up looks at more than 100 critters, such as snakes, mice, and raccoons. Young kids especially take to the petting corral, where they can stroke rabbits and ducks. Staff members give free animal talks on Saturday.

The museum has put together a strong program for families. Year-round, the Randall offers nature and art classes for all ages (registration required) that last 8–10 weeks for one hour per week. Art classes might include woodworking, ceramics, and jewelry making; nature classes might focus on biology or the environment. The Randall also hosts drop-in Saturday workshops for families. The Randall Theatre has concerts, films, and performances. Pick up a schedule at the museum for details.

If you like this sight you may also like the Bay Area Discovery Museum (#61).

EATS FOR KIDS There are no eating places in the immediate vicinity of the museum, so plan to either bring picnic food to Corona Heights Park or search out restaurants in adjoining neighborhoods. If you approach the Randall from the Haight-Ashbury district, check out the **Pork Store Café** (1451 Haight St., tel. 415/864–6981), where you can dig in to great breakfasts and big sandwiches. A few blocks east down the hill from the museum in the Castro District, **Sparky's Diner** (242 Church St., tel. 415/626–8666) serves diner-style breakfasts as well as burgers and fries.

KEEP IN MIND Corona Heights Park is a great climb, but be aware that kids gather here to party at night and some homeless crash here, leaving broken bottles and the occasional needle around. Keep younger kids close so you don't get a nasty shock when your child says "Hey mama, look what I found!"

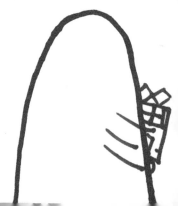

SAN FRANCISCO BAY
NATIONAL WILDLIFE REFUGE

Just north of San Jose on the southern reaches of San Francisco Bay, this was the country's first urban wildlife refuge, founded in 1972, and it's still one of the most popular—both with wildlife and humans. With 23,000 protected acres along 25 miles of shoreline, the refuge has an extensive system of boardwalks and trails for hiking and cycling, from which you can view potentially hundreds of wildlife species in the salt ponds, marshes, and mudflats. During fall and spring migrations, it's a way station for more than a million shorebirds, waterfowl, and wading birds: sandpipers, peregrine falcons, snowy egrets, great blue herons, canvasback ducks, mallards, kites, terns, and brown pelicans. Harbor seals also often hang around.

KEEP IN MIND Unless your kids are big birders or have an interest in formations like salt ponds, they're likely to just happily run along the trails. This can be plenty of fun, but there are many places closer to the city to do it.

Administered by the U.S. Fish and Wildlife Service, the refuge is part of a large complex of U.S.-run refuges in the Bay Area, including the Farallon National Wildlife Refuge (#46). Stop at the visitor center to see exhibits, use the observation deck, and pick up trail information. Several trailheads are nearby. The best for kids is the Tidelands Trail, which

MAKE THE MOST OF YOUR TIME Especially if you're coming all the way from San Francisco, you might want to combine a visit here with other family-friendly attractions in the area. Ardenwood Historic Farm (#63) is a living-history treasure only a mile or so away. Also nearby is a nice East Bay park, Coyote Hills (8000 Patterson Ranch Rd., Fremont, tel. 510/795–9385), which has picnic facilities, wetlands (including a marsh boardwalk), naturalist programs, and hiking and biking trails. Try the 3½-mile Bay View Trail.

Visitor center, 1 Marshlands Rd., Fremont; education center, 1751 Grand Blvd., Alviso

 Free

 Daily sunrise–sunset, visitor center
T–Su 10–5, education center
T–F 8–4, Sa–Su 10–5

510/792-0222 visitor center,
408/262-5513 education center;
desfbay.fws.gov

6 and up

meanders up and down a hill, along the shoreline, and across footbridges for 1⅓ miles. A dozen more miles of trails, as well as more displays and an observation deck, are found several miles away at the refuge's Environmental Education Center, near the town of Alviso; call for directions, which are complicated, or pick up a map at the visitor center. Inner Baird Island is a less-used portion of the refuge (with one trail), across the Dumbarton Bridge near the town of Redwood City, on the western side of San Francisco Bay.

The refuge offers two-hour weekend family nature hikes (call or check the Web site for a schedule) as well as summer day camps and an annual Kids' Night Out, which includes campfire stories, nature walks, and stargazing programs. But the real treat is what you'll see here just about any day of the year.

If you like this sight you may also like Coyote Point Park and Museum (#49), the Marin Headlands (#31), and Point Reyes National Seashore (#18).

EATS FOR KIDS Some picnic facilities lie along the Tidelands Trail near the visitor center, and a few picnic tables are adjacent to the education center, but you must pack out your trash. For information about restaurants near the visitor center *see #63.*

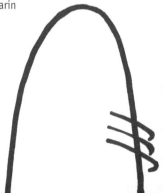

SAN FRANCISCO FIRE DEPARTMENT MUSEUM

I f your kids have ever dreamed of being firefighters, bring them to this small museum in Pacific Heights crammed full of firefighting memorabilia. Brave firefighters have been battling blazes in San Francisco for more than 150 years, and the museum traces their colorful history, from Gold Rush days through the 1906 earthquake to more modern times.

Glass cases display artifacts ranging from helmets and ribbons to buckets and uniforms. There's also an array of old photos and press clippings from famous fires and tributes to fire chiefs and Lillie Coit (#50), the city's number-one fire buff. But it's the antique firefighting equipment that most fascinates kids. The city was growing rapidly during the Gold Rush in 1850, when a dozen or so rowdy volunteer firefighting groups first banded together to try to save the town's shacklike residences from burning down. Among their equipment were hand pumps that required up to 16 men to operate; one, built prior to 1849, is on display here. A few years later, the firefighting teams were professionals, but they still dragged hose carts themselves (being too macho to use horses); you can see one

MAKE THE MOST OF YOUR TIME Ask the museum's volunteer guide if it's okay to peek inside the real fire station (No. 10) next door. Chances are, if the fire bells aren't ringing just then, you and your kids can get permission to look around and see the latest in firefighting technology.

655 Presidio Ave.

415/558-3546 recording, 415/563-4630
voice; www.sffiremuseum.org

Free

Th-Su 1-4

4 and up

of those, too. An 1893 La France steam engine on wheels, also on display, helped replace the hand-drawn hose carts.

It's easy to overlook some little gems here, among them an original fire bell from Portsmouth Square (in Chinatown), which rang for the last time on April 18, 1906—the day of the great San Francisco earthquake and fire. Another is a small exhibit about the city's 150-year-old firebox alarm system, which operated essentially like a telegraph. Now here's the kicker: The system is still in use, with hundreds of the alarm boxes remaining on the streets. Except these days, since almost all fires are reported by phone, the boxes usually ring false alarms (schoolkids take note).

If you like this sight you may also like the Oakland Museum of California (#23).

KEEP IN MIND
This is a small museum—though it's loaded with tons of tiny treasures—and you're likely to get through quickly. You're also likely to be the only visitors, so chat up the volunteer on duty. These guys love firefighting and will be happy to share information and regale you with tales of fighting flames.

EATS FOR KIDS Just down the street from the museum, **Ella's** (500 Presidio Ave., tel. 415/441-5669) serves classic American cooking, including great pancake breakfasts and meat-loaf dinners, amid casual but attractive surroundings. Around the corner in the Laurel Village shopping plaza, **Pasta Pomodoro** (3611 California St., tel. 415/831-0900) turns out tasty, inexpensive pasta dishes. A block north in the Sacramento Street shopping district, casual **Picnix Bistro & Carry Out** (3872 Sacramento St., tel. 415/751-2255) has great American and Vietnamese sandwiches (try the Saigon chicken) to stay or take out.

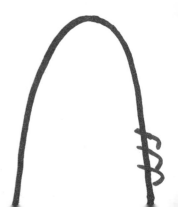

SAN FRANCISCO MAIN LIBRARY

The city's top library, which moved into a new building in 1996, can be quite entertaining, starting with the talking elevators. As you ride, a voice calls out helpful information like "going up," "please turn right," and "first floor." But then libraries are full of helpful information, and this is one of the most technologically advanced in the country. It has some 300 computer terminals, many with free Internet access and CD-ROM capability; sizable video and music collections; and, of course, a good many books. You can enjoy all this in an architecturally striking, modern building that's airy and light and has plenty of open space.

At the Fisher Children's Center, on the second floor, librarians expect kids to be noisy, and the atmosphere is anything but stuffy. Here you'll find the Electronic Discovery Center, loaded with computers where your children can read stories or play video games. If you fear they'll do too much of the latter at the expense of the former, you may accompany them to explore what's available. Each child is allowed one 30-minute session per day, and then they have to go on a waiting list for another 30 minutes.

KEEP IN MIND Outside the Fisher Children's Center, entertaining exhibits often grab kids' attention even before they step inside. Some of these, such as an elaborate Thomas the Tank Engine Christmas train, are worth a visit on their own. Call the library to see what's on.

EATS FOR KIDS The small but pleasant **Library Café** (tel. 415/437–4838), on the lower level, has sandwiches, salads, and soups at reasonable prices. **Max's at the Opera** (601 Van Ness Ave., tel. 415/771–7300) serves sandwiches and other meals with portions big enough for a small family to share. Don't be surprised if your server, who may be an aspiring opera singer, breaks into song in the evening. **Pagolac** (655 Larkin St., tel. 415/776–3234) has fantastic Vietnamese noodle soups, seafood, and roll-your-own summer rolls in cool, casual surroundings. The area can be a bit questionable at night but it's fine for a lunchtime excursion.

Connected to the Electronic Discovery Center is a children's reading and story room. On Saturday morning at 11, story times for families of preschoolers last about ½ hour. On some weekdays story times are at 10:30. In another room, your kids can watch scheduled movies and learn crafts. Teenagers should check out the third-floor Teen Center, where books are geared to their age group. Elsewhere, you'll find collections of San Francisco memorabilia, an African-American Center, an Asian-American Center, and special art and photo exhibitions. A roof garden and terrace on the sixth floor is for all to use. If you want your family to get a sense of what's where, take one of the monthly tours, most suitable for fourth graders and up. But as soon as your kids spot the computers and other enticements here, they may want to desert the tour anyway. It's a place where they'll quickly discover that learning can be fun.

If you like this sight you may also like the California Academy of Sciences (#57), the Lawrence Hall of Science (#36), and Zeum at Yerba Buena Gardens (#1).

MAKE THE MOST OF YOUR TIME Across the

street in the Civic Center Plaza, a playground for elementary schoolkids, contains tire swings, slides, and monkey bars. City Hall, with its gleaming copper dome, is across the plaza and houses a small exhibit from the (currently homeless) Museum of the City of San Francisco, in the South Light Court. Open weekdays 8–8, it has nice exhibits about San Francisco's earthquakes—including the gigantic, iron head of the Goddess of Liberty statue that sat atop City Hall until the 1906 quake.

SAN FRANCISCO MUSEUM OF MODERN ART

It's true that few kids (or parents, for that matter) can tell abstract expressionism from analytical cubism, or surrealism from op art. And as for Dada, he's with Mama. But children are often drawn to the frequently bright colors, abstract figures, and geometric shapes of 20th-century art. The San Francisco Museum of Modern Art—or SF-MOMA—is now the country's second-largest modern art museum.

Opened in 1995 across from the Yerba Buena Center for the Arts, the bright, airy, six-story museum is topped by a 145-foot-tall skylight tower. The permanent collections—15,000 pieces, only a small portion of them displayed at one time—highlight painting and sculpture from 1900 to 1970. Picasso, Braque, Klee, Dalí, Matisse, Pollock, de Kooning, Rivera, and Kahlo are all here. Architecture and design, 20th-century photography (by Man Ray and Ansel Adams, among others), and special exhibits are also featured, along with video, audio, and interactive media installations—ranging from "weird" to "awesome" in the words of some young visitors. Computer screens scattered about the museum are designed

MAKE THE MOST OF YOUR TIME As the museum acknowl-
edges, some artworks have "challenging content or explicit imagery" and may not be appropriate for children. If this is a concern for you, preview the museum yourself before bringing
the kids. That way, you'll know which rooms (if any) to avoid. When a big show is on, you
might be in for crowds and a long wait. Time your visit accordingly: Some may be worth the
extra hassle to you and others won't. With young children, head straight upstairs to the temporary exhibits—many of which are large-scale and striking—and work your way back down.

151 3rd St.

415/357–4000, 415/947–1292
family programs; www.sfmoma.org

 $12.50 adults, $7 students 13 and up; Th 6–9 half-price; 1st T of mth free

 Memorial Day–Labor Day, F–T 10–6, Th 10–9; early Sept–late May, F–T 11–6, Th 11–9

6 and up

to help kids "make sense of modern art." For most kids, the highlight of a visit here is walking across the top floor's Turret Bridge, a narrow strip suspended three flights above the ground. At one end you'll be greeted by the shocking and/or amusing life-size ceramic statue of Michael Jackson and his monkey. The Museum Store, open daily, is superb, complete with a wonderful selection of children's art books and educational toys. Your kids can try out some toys on the spot, and you can shop without paying museum admission.

On some spring and summer Saturdays, parents and young children can explore color and form together in a program called Children's Art Studio. The seven one-hour sessions, also at the Koret Education Center, are for ages 2½–4 and 4–6.

If you like this sight you may also like the Mission District Murals (#25).

EATS FOR KIDS **Caffè Museo** (tel. 415/357–4500), on the ground floor of the museum, serves unusually tasty soups, focaccia sandwiches, and morning pastries; it's open during museum hours, including Thursday evenings. **Buca di Beppo** (855 Howard St., tel. 415/543–7673) is a boisterous, fun Italian restaurant with huge portions. The biggest collection of nearby restaurants is at Yerba Buena Gardens (#1), especially the food court area on the main floor of Metreon, where you can get everything from burritos and burgers to Asian-style noodles.

KEEP IN MIND In spite of your best planning, kids can get antsy in these hushed halls. If yours do, take advantage of the museum's in-and-out privileges and head right across the street to the Yerba Buena Gardens for a running and shouting break without the withering stares.

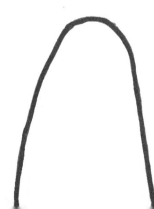

SAN FRANCISCO ZOO

In the midst of a massive renovation—half is done already—the "New Zoo" gives kids a startlingly close-up view of spectacular animals like grizzly bears and hippos in natural-looking environments, and parents will appreciate the lush, beautifully maintained setting. Set on 125 acres in the fog beltway near the ocean, this is Northern California's largest zoo, home to more than 1,000 birds and 220 species of animals.

With younger kids, start at the 7-acre Children's Zoo, near the front entrance, where they can peer at creepy crawlies in the indoor Insect Zoo and not only pet farm animals in the Barnyard, but maybe help out with grooming or collect newly laid eggs. At the meerkat and prairie dog exhibit here, kids can crawl through a prairie dog tunnel.

KEEP IN MIND If you and your family are San Francisco residents, you qualify for sizeable discounts on zoo admission. Adults get $2 off, youths $3.50 off, and children $2.50 off. Be sure to bring a picture ID that has your address written on it.

You can tour the main zoo's blockbuster exhibits on a big loop. Start off at the Lemur Forest, where ring-tailed and red ruffed lemurs swing through trees and lie on their backs like big cats. Next door in the Primate Discovery Center, colobus and patas monkeys,

MAKE THE MOST OF YOUR TIME Kids can hear what it's like to be a zookeeper straight from the horse's mouth. Year-round on weekends and daily in summer, learn what meerkats and prairie dogs like to eat, what defense mechanisms insects have, and what kinds of animals are native to North America. Plenty of special talks happen in summer, so be sure to ask at the gate when you enter.

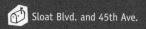

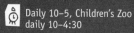

white ruffed lemurs, and macaques live and play in a spectacular bi-level setting. The interactive learning exhibits on the ground level are ideal for school-age kids. Then check out the chimps and the anteaters on the way to the far end of the zoo, which houses the absolute don't-miss Grizzly Gulch exhibit. Here orphaned sisters Kachina and Kiona enchant visitors with their frolicking and swimming. Small kids tend to like Penguin Island, where dozens of Magellanic penguins dive into a 200-foot pool; the penguins are fed daily at 3.

There are even nonanimal activities here. Your kids can ride the carousel ($2; free for standing adults) or the Little Puffer miniature steam train ($3), and check out the playground near the Children's Zoo. The Wildlife Theatre stages shows late June–Labor Day, where kids can see live, uncaged animals like opossums and turtles.

If you like this sight you may also like the California Academy of Sciences (#57).

EATS FOR KIDS The zoo has four casual cafés, including the Leaping Lemur Café, just up the hill from the carousel, and the Playfield Café, near the playground and Children's Zoo, where you can get hot dogs, ice cream, and the like. After you're done at the zoo, head toward the ocean a bit to find John's Ocean Beach Cafe (2898 Sloat Blvd., tel. 415/665–8292), which serves breakfast all day as well as lunches of burgers, sandwiches, omelets, and soups.

SANTA CRUZ BEACH BOARDWALK

Set alongside a wide, sandy beach about 75 miles south of San Francisco, the Santa Cruz Beach Boardwalk is the largest full-scale seaside amusement park remaining on the West Coast. Operating since 1907, it now draws 3 million visitors annually. It's a place where you can come and go as you please—strolling down the boardwalk is free—and pay for rides as you take them. Unlike many modern theme parks, the atmosphere is far from antiseptic; carnival-style games and food stands selling corn dogs and cotton candy add an air of old-fashioned funkiness and nostalgia.

For kids, though, the big draw is rides, rides, and more rides, 34 in all, some appropriate for every age group past infant. Kids ages 8 and above, and brave younger ones, head for the Giant Dipper, a classic wooden coaster that's been declared a National Historic Landmark. Less-adventurous kids can cut their coaster teeth on the smaller Sea Serpent. The Haunted Castle, a dark ride where monsters jump out at you as you pass, is relatively tame but could frighten tots. The Logger's Revenge, a log flume ride with a steep plunge at the end, is a

MAKE THE MOST OF YOUR TIME Check online for discount coupons for rides and attractions; sometimes a group of passes. From mid-May through October, you can ride to the Beach Boardwalk and back on the Santa Cruz Big Trees & Pacific Railway, which operates on a historic track that runs through Henry Cowell Redwoods State Park, down a scenic river gorge, across a 1909 steel truss bridge, and through an 1875 tunnel. Trains leave from Roaring Camp, 6 miles north of Santa Cruz in Felton, or you can start at the boardwalk. Either way, riding time is one hour. Call 831/335–4484 or visit the Web site at www.roaringcamp.com for prices and schedules.

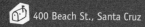

good way to get wet on a hot day. Bumper cars and a Ferris wheel are other favorites, as is the Sky Glider, an overhead chair lift that travels high over the park. The height could scare young kids. Tots who want to avoid all of the above can take a spin on the ornate 1911 Looff carousel, with its 73 hand-carved horses. Nine kiddie rides, including Jet Copters, Sea Dragons, and Kiddie Bumper Boats, add to the fun.

You can even find entertainment here on rainy days. The boardwalk's indoor attractions include a large video arcade and Neptune's Kingdom, a two-story minigolf course complete with talking pirates, firing cannons, and an erupting volcano. But the main action is outdoors, where salt fills the air, waves crash in the background, and you feel like you've entered a time warp back to an old-time seaside carnival.

If you like this sight you may also like Paramount's Great America (#20).

EATS FOR KIDS Some 30 food vendors line the boardwalk, dispensing treats such as corn dogs, pizza, burgers, nachos, funnel cake, Dippin' Dots (ice cream), garlic fries, clam chowder, and saltwater taffy. If you're in search of a sit-down place, head for the **Dolphin Restaurant** (tel. 831/426–5830), at the end of the Municipal Pier near the boardwalk. It serves seafood lunches and dinners (along with big breakfasts) amid casual decor and water views. A kids' menu includes fish-and-chips and, of course, corn dogs. Note that the prices are much lower if you order at the window and eat outside on the benches.

KEEP IN MIND The boardwalk is serious teen territory, especially in the evenings. Kids are generally well behaved, but you're likely to hear some colorful language and see fairly open displays of affection. City kids generally don't bat an eye, but if you're on the sensitive side or have only younger children, you'll want to stick to family attractions and head out before dinner.

SIX FLAGS DISCOVERY KINGDOM

9

The theme of this ambitious combination wildlife park, oceanarium, and amusement park, all packed into 135 acres about 35 miles northeast of San Francisco, is "the best of land, sea, and sky." So if your children want to feed a giraffe, commune with dolphins, or ride a roller coaster, they can do it here.

The Dolphin Harbor stadium provides a slick showcase for bottlenose dolphins, who jump 20 feet out of the water and do tail walks, flips, air spins, and other "behaviors" (what we used to call "tricks"). If you crave more interaction, the new two-hour Dolphin Discovery program, for those 48" and up, allows you to meet and greet dolphins in the water; it's given daily in summer and Wednesday–Sunday during other seasons, will set you back a hefty $150 a person (which includes park admission), and requires reservations (tel. 707/556-5274). Probably the park's most popular show stars Shouka the Killer Whale; be sure to arrive early. The Tiger Island Splash Attack provides an underwater view of a dozen

KEEP IN MIND Though plenty of parents of younger children bring their kids here, considering the expense, there are many cheaper, equally entertaining options for little ones.

MAKE THE MOST OF YOUR TIME A few tips can make your visit cheaper and smoother. If you buy your tickets in advance at area Longs Drugstores, you can get substantial discounts on adult fares and not have to wait through long entrance lines. If you plan to visit more than once per year, a season pass ($80) can save big bucks. When you arrive, pick up a daily schedule, and plan your itinerary to make sure you cover as many shows, rides, and attractions as you can fit in. The shows are offered at various times throughout the day, and good seats often go early.

Bengal tigers at play. Little ones recognize old friends like Bugs Bunny and Daffy Duck in the Looney Tunes Talent Show.

Animal exhibits include the riveting Shark Experience, where you'll move along a ramp through a clear tunnel in a huge shark tank. At Giraffe Dock, your kids can hand-feed the giraffes. At Elephant Encounter, they can play tug-of-war with an elephant; you can also ride elephants for an extra fee.

If your kids are into roller coasters, they'll find plenty to keep them screaming here. Rides range from the V-2 Vertical Velocity—which travels forward, backward, and up and down two 150-foot-tall sky towers at 70 mph—to a Ferris wheel and a river-rapids ride.

If you like this sight you may also like the Santa Cruz Beach Boardwalk (#10).

EATS FOR KIDS Concessions at the park include **Seamoore Cott's Fish and Chips** (also chicken strips) and **Outback Burgers** (for burgers and fries), both of which have outdoor tables. The **Carnivore Café** has ribs and chicken, and the **Lost Temple Café** features corn dogs. For dessert, head to **Ben & Jerry's** or **Fresh Mini Donuts & More**—watch them made—and there are a number of snack stands, too. To save money, you can bring your own picnic food (no glass bottles or alcohol) to eat at tables near Lakeside Plaza and Shark Experience.

STERN GROVE FESTIVAL

Every parent knows that taking young kids to an indoor concert can be a kicking, squirming disaster. This outdoor music festival series offers a chance to introduce children to a variety of musical styles—even opera and symphony—without the worry or the cost. Sigmund Stern Grove—a recently renovated 33-acre stand of eucalyptus, redwood, and fir trees in the Sunset District—provides a shady setting and natural amphitheater for the nation's oldest free outdoor concert series. Running annually since 1937 and drawing about 100,000 people per season, it's one of the city's arts treasures.

The grove, a gift to the city from the widow of a local civic and business leader, extends down steep hillsides to a valley, where a grassy meadow looks up to a stage. Some unreserved bench seating is available directly in front of the stage; the most select seating includes picnic tables available by reservation (also free) for a maximum party of six (call 415/831–5500 at 9 AM on the Monday preceding the concert). Most of the audience stretches out or sits on the grass, while latecomers can find perches on the tree-lined hillsides

MAKE THE MOST OF YOUR TIME To pass the time while waiting for the concert, bring the Sunday paper, some toys or books for the kids, and plenty of snacks. A small playground (partially hidden by trees), just inside the 19th Avenue entrance on the Sloat Boulevard side of Stern Grove, can help entertain younger kids. And come prepared for changes in the weather as the day goes by. It's often sunny early on, so bring plenty of sunscreen. But dress everyone in layers, because Stern Grove frequently gets chilly by mid-afternoon, when the summertime fog rolls in.

19th Ave. and Sloat Blvd.

 Donations accepted

 Mid-June–mid-Aug, Su 2

415/252–6252 recording, 415/252–6253 voice; www.sterngrove.org

5 and up

to the rear, which are decidedly less comfortable. The ideal approach is to bring a picnic lunch, arrive early (no later than noon, and by midmorning for a good view), and spread a blanket or set low-slung lawn chairs out on the grass. At noon before each concert, kids can participate in engaging art-related activities at KidStage. They might make Mardi Gras masks, join a drum circle, or explore instruments at a rock-and-roll petting zoo, but any of these fun hands-on programs will help them blow off some steam before the show starts. Then sit back and enjoy the performance.

If you like this sight you may also like the Golden Gate Park Band summer Sunday concerts (#41) and the Yerba Buena Gardens Festival (#1).

KEEP IN MIND

Having a great time at Stern Grove depends hardly at all on who's playing, so consider packing a picnic and spending the day even if your children don't express any interest in Cuban jazz, opera, or sitar music.

EATS FOR KIDS Picnics are the most fun. If you don't bring food, several **concession stands** set up shop during the concerts, serving such items as burgers, knishes, and ice-cream bars. After the performance, head to the lively restaurant scene in nearby West Portal. Terrific thin-crust pizza and house-made everything are on the menu at casual **Paradise Pizza & Pasta** (393 W. Portal Ave., tel. 415/759–1155). For good Mexican food amid decor riotous enough to keep the kids' attention, try **El Toreador Restaurant** (50 W. Portal Ave., tel. 415/566–8104).

TECH MUSEUM OF INNOVATION

Loaded with custom-designed interactive exhibits, the Tech Museum is devoted solely to the innovations in microelectronics, communications, robotics, and biotechnology that have emerged in Silicon Valley. The description may be a mouthful, but this museum does a great job helping to demystify technology and make it fun for kids—and their parents. The Tech's 132,000-square-foot, mango-and-azure domed facility in the heart of downtown houses some 250 cutting-edge exhibits arranged in four theme areas, and they're meant not just to inform and entertain, but to inspire museum visitors of all ages to be innovative themselves.

Activities go beyond "hands-on" to "minds-on," as museum staffers put it. In the Life Tech gallery, you and your kids can "drive" a simulated bobsled, use sound waves to "see" inside yourself, or enter images of a human body for an inside look. The Life Tech Theatre presents shows that entertainingly illuminate high-tech themes. In the Innovation gallery, you can visit a "cleanroom" to see how microchips (the stuff of Silicon Valley) are made,

EATS FOR KIDS The museum's **Café Primavera** (tel. 408/885–1094) has both indoor and outdoor seating. Sandwiches, salads, pizzas, and pastas are reasonably priced. Nearby, at the landmark Fairmont Hotel, the **Fountain at the Fairmont** (170 S. Market St., tel. 408/998–1900) serves breakfast, lunch, and dinner; casual dress is fine.

KEEP IN MIND An unusually cool feature here is the Tech Tag, a bar-coded strip for each visitor that allows you to take pictures of yourself at work at certain exhibits. These photos are uploaded to your own private space on the museum's Web page, so kids get a cyber scrapbook of their visit (and subsequent visits if they save the card). Though the Tech does have a section just for small children, most exhibits are aimed at kids about 9 and up—they're complex ideas explained with lots of text, and the hands-on elements can be complicated. If you do bring little kids, don't miss the Imagination Station's Shadow Catcher.

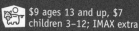

create your own futuristic bike design, and take an actual portrait of yourself with a laser scanner. The Exploration gallery has some of the most exciting stuff for kids about 5 and up, even those not really into science. Here you can probe the ocean depths with an underwater, remote-controlled robot; control a moon rover; sit in a jet-pack chair to test your ability to move around while weightless (as in a spaceship); and stand on the earthquake platform to feel the vertical and horizontal jerks of a major quake. The museum's Hackworth IMAX Dome Theater has a hemispherical screen 82 feet in diameter. Call for tickets or order from the Web site in advance, as demand is high.

The museum also hosts traveling exhibits, such as Gunter von Hagens' controversial *Body Worlds*, an anatomical exhibition of real human bodies (minus the skin); these sometimes require additional admission fees.

If you like this sight you may also like the Exploratorium (#47).

MAKE THE MOST OF YOUR TIME Try to get

here early; you'll face more crowds, but some exhibits close before the museum does. San Jose has other good museums for kids. One of the country's largest interactive kids' museums, the Children's Discovery Museum of San Jose (180 Woz Way, tel. 408/298–5437), whose outer walks are painted Easter-egg purple, is chock-full of hands-on exhibits geared to ages 2–12. Meanwhile, San Jose's Rosicrucian Egyptian Museum (1342 Naglee Ave., tel. 408/947–3636), contains a fascinating collection of mummies.

TILDEN PARK

Tilden Park is the East Bay's answer to San Francisco's Golden Gate Park. With more than 2,000 acres, it's about twice the size of its better-known cousin across the bay, and its grassy lawns, rolling hills, and eucalyptus and pine groves are full of recreation and picnic areas. Two lakes and peaks that rise to nearly 2,000 feet add form to the landscape. Woodsy hiking and biking trails lead throughout, and family attractions dot the park.

Tilden is particularly strong on activities for younger kids. At the Little Farm, kids can pet and feed sheep, rabbits, cows, pigs, and pygmy goats. The farm has a little barn and windmill, and ducks and geese paddle in the pond. It's open 8:30–3:30 daily and costs nothing; be sure to bring lettuce or celery to feed the animals. Elsewhere in the park, you'll find a 1911 antique Herschel-Spillman merry-go-round with hand-carved animals and a calliope and the Tilden Park Steam Train, which chugs along a scenic ridge. These are open on weekends and during school vacations.

MAKE THE MOST OF YOUR TIME The park's Environmental Education Center (tel. 510/525–2233), near the Little Farm, offers hiking, nature, and other special programs for kids and families year-round. You can study the life of a pond, learn how to make sushi, or attend a free concert. Some programs require reservations, and some require fees (usually $5–$25), so drop by or call for a schedule. The Environmental Education Center also has an interactive exhibit about nearby Wildcat Creek (just north of Tilden) that kids might enjoy.

Families with kids of any age can enjoy the park's Lake Anza, which has a sandy beach that's popular for swimming (May–October). The water is generally sun warmed and sheltered from the wind by hills, and lifeguards are on duty in season. You can also fish in the lake throughout the year.

The park's eastern edge is well suited to families with older children. Here the East Bay Skyline National Recreation Trail winds along the crests of hills to Inspiration Point. The trail is accessible to hikers, horseback riders, and cyclists (the latter on fire road portions only) and links Tilden to other regional parks. Views stretch across the metropolitan Bay Area. Tilden also contains an 18-hole public golf course and driving range and a botanic garden featuring the world's most complete collection of native California plants.

If you like this sight you may also like Ardenwood Historic Farm (#63).

KEEP IN MIND In December, the park's carousel lights up with a delightful display. Sparkling, large-scale decorations pack the lawn outside; Christmas trees decorated to the hilt surround the spinning carousel; and squirming kids pose with Santa and sip hot chocolate between rides. Little eyes grow wide on the drive up, past some spectacular Berkeley Hills homes alight with seasonal spirit.

EATS FOR KIDS
The park has numerous picnic areas, as well as concession stands at Lake Anza, the merry-go-round, and other locations.

U.S.S. HORNET

5

Rising out of the bay like a behemoth floating city and flanked by gigantic navy freighters with towering cranes, the aircraft carrier U.S.S. *Hornet* will make you feel like one tiny sailor indeed. Standing as high as two blue whales stacked nose to tail, the navy vessel, launched in 1943, gives kids a close-up view of military aircraft from World War II through the Gulf War; a glimpse into the labyrinthine, tightly packed world of sailors; and the chance to return to the time when humans first walked on the moon.

Visitors climb a steepish ramp to board the carrier, and enter on the hangar deck, which houses a decent collection of military aircraft. Kids are often most impressed with the F-14 Tomcat, just like the ones flown in *Top Gun* (and the only plane here too big to fly off the carrier); with a docent, you can climb the steep stairs to peek into the Tomcat's cramped cockpit. The other aircraft here—including the cool A-4 Skyhawk with its mid-air refueling arm in place, the FJ-2 Fury 1950s fighter jet, and the H-34 Sea Horse Vietnam-era Marine helicopter—can only be viewed from the ground, and none can be boarded.

KEEP IN MIND Visiting the *Hornet* is hard with little ones: Ladders are many and steep, tours can be meandering and long-winded, some docents are anxious, and you'll see loads of "Do Not Touch" signs. If you have young children with you, forgo the tour and stick to the hangar deck itself.

MAKE THE MOST OF YOUR TIME The U.S.S. *Hornet* has a robust calendar of engaging programs, including living ship days, when aircraft are transported to the flight deck; flashlight tours (ages 12 and up, $35) that take in areas of the ship usually off limits; and family overnights (ages 5 and up, $100 per person). If you visit on the weekend, add a quick stop at the **Alameda Naval Air Museum** (2151 Ferry Point, tel. 510/522–4262), also in Alameda Point, with plane models, uniforms, and lots of documentation.

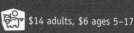

Also on the hangar deck, one of the most comprehensive exhibits on the carrier and one sure to be a hit with kids interested in space covers the Apollo 11 space capsule, in which the first astronauts to walk on the moon returned to earth. A Navy Sea King rescue helicopter launched from the U.S.S. *Hornet* recovered the capsule and returned the astronauts to the carrier, where they remained in quarantine in a hip-looking Gulfstream trailer. Kids can follow Neil Armstrong's footprints (painted on the floor) from the helicopter to the trailer and see one of the Apollo training capsules. Climb many ladders to the flight deck, where a plane or two usually sits with wings folded. Climb up to "the island"—the control tower—and visit the navigation bridge to see the gorgeous brass wheel used to steer the carrier. A docent can translate the lingo chart on the wall, explaining terms like "bingo" (coming in for a landing).

If you like this sight you may also like the Hiller Aviation Museum (#40).

EATS FOR KIDS The *Hornet* has a couple of vending machines to ward off low blood sugar, and **a concession stand** operates on weekends. Just outside Alameda Point, tiny and very casual **Everett & Jones Barbeque** (1930 Main St., tel. 510/814–6149) serves up renowned ribs in sweet smoky sauce. Alameda's main drag has many kid-friendly places; enjoy good Mexican food and decent drinks at colorfully decorated **Otaez** (1619 Webster St., tel. 510/521–9090). In Oakland's Chinatown, excellent Chinese and Vietnamese noodles are the specialty at **Vien Huong** (712 Franklin St., tel. 510/465–5938).

WATERWORLD CALIFORNIA

4

Though summer days are often cool and foggy in San Francisco, they can get positively scorching in Concord, 45 minutes or so to the east. And that's exactly where you'll find the water park nearest the city. Run by the Six Flags company, Waterworld California encompasses 20 acres of places to splash, slide, float, plunge, and dip.

Thirteen major rides and attractions cater to kids of all ages older than infants. On the Big Kahuna, the park's most popular slide, the entire family (up to six people) can shoot its way down on a raft. Toddlers and other tots head to Treasure Island, an interactive structure featuring waterfalls, fountains, water cannons, minislides, and tire swings. Wild Water Kingdom, a 20,000-square-foot activity pool, is the other big gathering place for preschoolers, with the Dragon's Tail slide complex in Tot Town and a lily pad walk.

Older kids also find excitement at Wild Water Kingdom thanks to the Diablo Falls Shotgun Slides, which end with a 6-foot free fall into a 10-foot-deep pool. Kids have to be 48" tall

MAKE THE MOST OF YOUR TIME Ordering tickets online may save you a few bucks, so check there first. You'll also avoid potentially long lines this way, but nothing will save you the $10 parking fee. You'll need to bring your own towels, and don't forget to pack dry clothes, sunscreen, sunglasses, hats, and beach shoes or sandals. You might also want to bring water toys for young kids. The park has a shop for purchasing such items, but not at bargain prices. If you arrive before the early-afternoon crush, you'll stand a better chance of finding a parking space and a lounge chair for relaxing in sun or shade when you're not in the pools.

1950 Waterworld Pkwy. (off I-680), Concord

 $29.99 48" and up,
$23.99 47" and under,
2 and under free

 Mid-May–Sept, days and hrs vary
(mid-June–Aug, daily)

925/609-1364;
www.waterworldcalifornia.com

3 and up

to ride this one, as they do on several others, including the Cliff Hanger, another slide that ends in a free fall. The Typhoon Double Tube Slides, on which you travel 4½ stories down four different slides, may be even more thrilling. On the equally high Honolulu Halfpipe, daring kids can ride a towering wave both forward and backward. Less-daring kids, and parents, can float leisurely on a tube down the Kaanapali Kooler, a 15-foot-wide, 1,000-foot-long river, or bodysurf or ride a tube through the waves at the huge Breaker Beach Wave Pool. Free life jackets are provided, as they are at Wild Water Kingdom. The park emphasizes safety, but accidents do happen—so keep a close eye on your kids, keep them lathered in sunscreen, and make sure youngsters stay out of the line of fire of cannonballing teens.

If you like this sight you may also like Adventure Playground (#68).

KEEP IN MIND

One adult is required to stay with each child 8 and under, so be sure you have enough adults to cover the kids. With water-park drownings in the news recently, look for life jacket recommendations to be changed to requirements.

EATS FOR KIDS No coolers, food, or beverages can be brought into the park (except for infants). You can, however, have lunch in a public picnic area on the northeast end of the parking lot and return to the park if you get your hand stamped. The park's concession stands include the **Windjammer Food Court,** which sells hot dogs, cheeseburgers, and curly fries, and the **Surf Side Grill,** which serves up Mexican meals and snacks. There's also an **ice-cream shop** and a **candy cabana.**

WELLS FARGO HISTORY MUSEUM

3

A museum off a bank lobby? Though that's a bit unusual, this little museum is well worth a detour to the Financial District. Wells Fargo began banking and express operations in San Francisco in 1852, just after the Gold Rush of 1849 lured thousands of treasure-seekers to California. The company delivered letters, safeguarded money and valuables, and bought, sold, and transported gold.

In 1861 the company ran the fabled Pony Express between Sacramento and Salt Lake City as part of the Pony Express's 10-day mail-delivery service between San Francisco and Missouri, a taxing and dangerous journey. The cost was 10¢ per ½ ounce (as opposed to 3¢ for a letter through the U.S. mail). By the late 1860s, Wells Fargo stagecoaches dominated overland mail and transportation in the West. So although the museum is in part a commercial for the West's oldest bank, it also documents a colorful slice of California history.

KEEP IN MIND If you've brought the kids here because they're into Gold Rush history, head west into the Jackson Square area. The center of the bawdy Barbary Coast, Jackson Square contains some of the city's oldest buildings—including the former home of Hotaling's Whiskey Distillery.

MAKE THE MOST OF YOUR TIME Though the Financial District, where the museum is located, isn't exactly a family mecca, it's an easy walk from both Chinatown and the Embarcadero (#51 and #48), so you can combine a visit here with some sightseeing in those neighborhoods. The museum is also near the California Street cable-car line. Forget driving here; parking is impossible during the museum's hours.

 420 Montgomery St.

415/396-2619;
www.wellsfargohistory.com/museums

Free

M–F 9–5

4 and up

Nicely presented exhibits cover two floors. As you enter, you'll see the 1867 Wells Fargo and Company Overland Stage Coach, one of 10 passenger coaches used in the company's route from the Bay Area to St. Louis. Payment got each of nine tightly packed passengers a "through-ticket and 15 inches of seat." Nearby, you'll find a re-created early-day Wells Fargo office—complete with telegraph (you can send messages back and forth between two desks using Morse Code), agent's desk, documents, treasure boxes, and package scales. Other exhibits focus on stagecoach drivers, the bandit-poet known as Black Bart, the Pony Express, and the Gold Rush. On the second floor, your kids can climb on a cutaway stagecoach seat, take the reins, and play driver. Nearby sits a coach (without wheels) that the entire family can squeeze into to get a feel for just how cramped—and no doubt hot and sticky—it got inside. There's also a first-floor general store where you can pick up souvenirs, such as gold-panning kits and model stagecoaches. The only thing you can't do is send a letter for 10¢.

If you like this sight you may also like the Cable Car Museum (#58).

EATS FOR KIDS Casual **Chez Carla** (200 Pine St., tel. 415/773-1220) makes wonderful sandwiches and has an impressive salad bar. Funky **Clown Alley** (Jackson St. and Columbus Ave., tel. 415/421-2540), a few blocks away, specializes in hamburgers and has both indoor and outdoor tables. For restaurants in nearby Chinatown, such as **Pearl City, Hang Ah,** and **Great Eastern,** see #51.

WINCHESTER MYSTERY HOUSE

Sarah Winchester's 160-room Victorian dwelling in San Jose is touted as the "world's oddest historical mansion," and you won't get many arguments on that. A wealthy widow—she was heiress to the Winchester rifle fortune—and devotee of the occult, Winchester began work on her house in 1884. After her husband and baby daughter died, Winchester apparently was convinced by a spiritualist that continuous building would appease the spirits of those killed by Winchester firearms and win eternal life for herself. That plan failed—she eventually died at age 82—but it certainly kept a platoon of carpenters employed. Following no discernible blueprints, they worked on the mansion 24 hours a day for the next 38 years, ending with her death in 1922.

The results are both beautiful and bizarre: Rooms with Tiffany glass windows, gold and silver chandeliers, inlaid doors, and parquet floors are juxtaposed with stairways and chimneys that lead nowhere, doors that open to blank walls, windows that are built into floors, and a layout so rambling and complex that the guides quip, "If you get separated

MAKE THE MOST OF YOUR TIME
Very young kids could get restless during the hour-long tour, and that presents some problems: Since you aren't allowed to wander on your own—you'd get lost—there's no way to bail out. Also note that strollers can't be accommodated; there are simply too many stairways and narrow passages. But for school-age kids and up, the tour can be remarkably compelling. The narration isn't confined to stuffy descriptions of house and family; it's jaunty and, like the tour itself, covers a lot of ground.

525 S. Winchester Blvd., San Jose

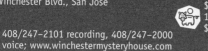 408/247-2101 recording, 408/247-2000 voice; www.winchestermysteryhouse.com

$20.95 to $28.95 ages 13 and up, $17.95 to $25.95 children 6-12

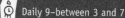 Daily 9-between 3 and 7

6 and up, behind-the-scenes and combined tours

from the group, there's no guarantee you'll ever be found." Even Winchester and her servants used maps to get around the bewildering maze.

The standard tour, a 1½-mile trek, lasts one hour, hitting the highlights as it passes through 110 rooms. A 55-minute, behind-the-scenes tour, good for return visitors, reveals the previously unseen workings of the estate, including the stables, a basement, and an unfinished ballroom. The downside of the latter tour for families is that kids under 10 aren't allowed on it for safety reasons (you have to wear hard hats, too). A Grand Estate tour combines the other two, for those who want to see every possible weird nook and cranny. You can also take self-guided tours of the extensive Victorian gardens and firearms museum, devoted mainly to the Winchester rifle, the "gun that won the West."

If you like this sight you may also like Alcatraz Island (#67).

EATS FOR KIDS You can relax after the tour at the **Winchester Café,** within the Mystery House, which serves snacks, desserts, and drinks. For good Mexican food, including fajitas with fresh tortillas as well as special kids' menus, check out the nearby branch of **Chevys** (550 S. Winchester Blvd., tel. 408/241-0158). The **Florentine** (745 S. Winchester Blvd., tel. 408/243-4040) has reasonably priced, traditional Italian food, such as pastas and pizzas, and a children's menu.

KEEP IN MIND If you're not sure your younger child(ren) will do well on the tour, save this destination for a few years. Once you've ventured into the house, there's nothing to do but stick with the guide around all the twists and turns, and doing it with a squirrelly kid is no fun.

YERBA BUENA GARDENS

Once a bleak industrial area, the South of Market blocks around—and above—the Moscone Convention Center have been transformed into a showplace of arts facilities, parks, and entertainment, all called Yerba Buena Gardens. Thanks to recent additions, it's now a premier family playground.

The Rooftop at Yerba Buena Gardens occupies 10 acres atop the largely underground Moscone Center South. Reached via a pedestrian bridge over Howard Street from the northern section of Yerba Buena Gardens, the Rooftop is loaded with activities geared to kids, though parents can play, too. A restored 1906-vintage Looff carousel, from the long-defunct Playland-at-the-Beach, is back in action. At Zeum, a high-tech interactive arts center, kids can create animation or a multimedia video. An NHL-size Ice Skating Center is San Francisco's only year-round public rink. Also here are a bowling alley and three landscaped acres with a Children's Garden and Play Circle, including a stream, slides, and child-size hedge maze.

MAKE THE MOST OF YOUR TIME Yerba Buena Gardens has some nice grassy spaces to just sit and relax. Best is the Esplanade, above Moscone Center North, which also has a terrace with outdoor cafés. The Martin Luther King Jr. Memorial Fountain includes a wide waterfall that children can scamper behind.

EATS FOR KIDS Adjacent to Zeum, **Mo's Gourmet Hamburgers** (772 Folsom St., tel. 415/957–3779), an outpost of a North Beach restaurant, has some outdoor tables. Metreon has several good eateries; grab takeout for a picnic in the gardens. Within the bustling first-floor food court, **Long Life Noodle Company** specializes in Asian-style noodles, and **Luna Azul** serves up burritos, quesadillas, and nachos. Other restaurants in the food court feature burgers, sushi, or desserts.

The Metreon, a futuristic shopping and entertainment Center, is adjacent to the parklands above Moscone Center North. It contains an IMAX theater along with 15 regular movie screens, plus an array of shops and restaurants. Many of the stores here appeal to kids, like Sony's PlayStation and Sony Style stores, the International Spy Shop, and Kamikaze POP, with its anime and manga products. Metreon also hosts blockbuster traveling shows, such as the *Titanic: The Artifact Exhibition* and *Leonardo DaVinci: An Exhibition of Genius*. From browsing the Metreon to playing on the rooftop, you'll find plenty of alternatives at this diverse, family-friendly entertainment complex.

If you like this sight you may also like Fisherman's Wharf (#45) and Golden Gate Park (#41).

KEEP IN MIND From May to October, the gardens host the Yerba Buena Gardens Festival (www.ybgf.org), a string of free afternoon and evening performances that runs the gamut from Latin jazz to theater. Within the festival, the Children's Garden Series features such entertainment as caterpillar puppets, African folk tales, and clowns.

CLASSIC GAMES

"I SEE SOMETHING YOU DON'T SEE AND IT IS BLUE." Stuck for a way to get your youngsters to settle down in a museum? Sit them down on a bench in the middle of a room and play this vintage favorite. The leader gives just one clue—the color—and everybody guesses away.

"I'M GOING TO THE GROCERY..." The first player begins, "I'm going to the grocery and I'm going to buy... " and finishes the sentence with the name of an object, found in grocery stores, that begins with the letter "A." The second player repeats what the first player has said, and adds the name of another item that starts with "B." The third player repeats everything that has been said so far and adds something that begins with "C" and so on through the alphabet. Anyone who skips or misremembers an item is out (or decide up front that you'll give hints to all who need 'em). You can modify the theme depending on where you're going that day, as "I'm going to X and I'm going to see..."

FAMILY ARK Noah had his ark—here's your chance to build your own. It's easy: Just start naming animals and work your way through the alphabet, from antelope to zebra.

PLAY WHILE YOU WAIT

NOT THE GOOFY GAME Have one child name a category. (Some ideas: first names, last names, animals, countries, friends, feelings, foods, hot or cold things, clothing.) Then take turns naming things that fall into that category. You're out if you name something that doesn't belong in the category—or if you can't think of another item to name. When only one person remains, start again. Choose categories depending on where you're going or where you've been—historic topics if you've seen a historic sight, animal topics before or after the zoo, upside-down things if you've been to the circus, and so on. Make the game harder by choosing category items in A-B-C order.

DRUTHERS How do your kids really feel about things? Just ask. "Would you rather eat worms or hamburgers? Hamburgers or candy?" Choose serious and silly topics—and have fun!

BUILD A STORY "Once upon a time there lived..." Finish the sentence and ask the rest of your family, one at a time, to add another sentence or two. Bring a tape recorder along to record the narrative—and you can enjoy your creation again and again.

GOOD TIMES GALORE

WIGGLE & GIGGLE Give your kids a chance to stick out their tongues at you. Start by making a face, then have the next person imitate you and add a gesture of his own—snapping fingers, winking, clapping, sneezing, or the like. The next person mimics the first two and adds a third gesture, and so on.

JUNIOR OPERA During a designated period of time, have your kids sing everything they want to say.

THE QUIET GAME Need a good giggle—or a moment of calm to figure out your route? The driver sets a time limit and everybody must be silent. The last person to make a sound wins.

BEST BETS

BEST IN TOWN
Alcatraz Island
Chinatown
Exploratorium
Golden Gate Park
Point Reyes National Seashore

BEST OUTDOORS
Point Reyes National Seashore

WACKIEST
Winchester Mystery House

BEST CULTURAL ACTIVITY
Chinatown

BEST MUSEUM
Exploratorium

SOMETHING FOR EVERYONE

ART ATTACK
Bay Area Discovery Museum **61**
Cartoon Art Museum **55**
Legion of Honor **35**
Murals of the Mission District **25**
Oakland Museum of California **23**
Randall Museum **16**
San Francisco Museum of Modern Art **12**

COOL 'HOODS
Chinatown **51**
Coit Tower and Telegraph Hill **50**
The Embarcadero **48**
Fisherman's Wharf **45**
Japantown **38**
Nob Hill **24**

CULTURE CLUB
Chinatown **51**
Japantown **38**
San Francisco Main Library **13**

FARMS AND ANIMALS
Año Nuevo State Reserve **65**
Aquarium of the Bay **64**
Ardenwood Historic Farm **63**

California Academy of Sciences **57**
Lindsay Wildlife Museum **33**
Oakland Zoo **22**
San Francisco Bay National Wildlife Refuge **15**
San Francisco Zoo **11**
Six Flags Discovery Kingdom **9**

FREEBIES
Adventure Playground **68**
Cable Car Museum **58**
China Beach **52**
Ft. Funston **44**
Ft. Point National Historic Site **43**
Golden Gate Park **41**
Ocean Beach **21**
Point Reyes National Seashore **18**
Presidio National Park **17**
Stern Grove Festival **8**

GAMES AND AMUSEMENTS
Children's Fairyland **53**
Paramount's Great America **20**
Pier 39 **19**

ALL AROUND TOWN

MANY THANKS!

Acknowledgements for the first and second editions:

To my parents, Clark and Mary Norton, with loving thanks, who introduced me to San Francisco when I was 9. For providing invaluable information, assistance, and suggestions for this book, the author would like to thank Laurie Armstrong; Helen Chang; Timothy Chanaud; David Perry; Susan Wilson; Jan Bollwinkel-Smith; Al Sassus; Nick and Esther Baran; Mel, Emily, and Natalie Flores; Mimi Sarkisian; Pat and Anne Forte; Michael and Beth Ward; Michael and Mary Reiter; Veronica Daly; Sheldon Clark; Tom and Chris Sonnemann; Bob Siegel; Pat Koren; Mary Viviano; Lana Beckett; and my most faithful researchers and travel companions, Catharine, Grael, and Lia Norton. I'm also grateful to my ever-supportive and instructive editors at Fodor's, with special thanks to Andrea Lehman.

—Clark Norton

Acknowledgments for the third edition:

For my sons, Jasper and Lukas, who are always up for another San Francisco experience, especially if it involves a bakery.

—Denise M. Leto